Mastering Candlestick Chart Patterns

Elio Vazquez

In the dynamic and ever-evolving world of trading, success often hinges on making informed decisions quickly and accurately. Among the myriad tools available to traders, candlestick chart patterns are one of the most powerful and versatile techniques for analyzing market movements. Their unique ability to convey a wealth of information in a compact, visual format makes them indispensable for novice and seasoned traders.

A Journey Towards Trading Mastery

Trading is as much an art as it is a science. While technical knowledge is vital, successful trading also requires intuition, experience, and emotional control. This book aims to equip you with the technical skills needed to read and understand candlestick charts, as well as the strategic insights to apply this knowledge effectively in real-world trading situations.

By the end of this book, you will not only be able to recognize key candlestick patterns but also understand their implications and how to leverage them to enhance your trading performance. Embark on this journey with us, and take a significant step towards mastering the art of trading with candlestick chart patterns.

Let's Begin

Turn the page and start your journey into the fascinating world of candlestick chart patterns. Your path to becoming a more informed, strategic, and successful trader begins here.

LET'S TALK ABOUT

MASTERING CANDLESTICK CHART PATTERNS

A COMPREHENSIVE GUIDE
TO TRADING STRATEGIES

FOR STOCK TRADERS

BY ELIO VAZQUEZ

Copyright Notice:

All rights reserved. No part of this book may be reproduced, distributed, or transmitted in any form or by any means, including photocopying, recording, or other electronic or mechanical methods, without the prior written permission of the author, except in the case of brief quotations embodied in critical reviews and certain other noncommercial uses permitted by copyright law.

This book is also published in a variety of electronic formats. Some content that appears in print may not be available in electronic books.

For permission requests, please contact the author at the following address:
Elio Vazquez
7990 SW 117th Ave, Suite 133
Miami, FL 33183-3845
support@eliovazquez.com

Contact Information:
If you have any questions about this book, please contact the author at support@eliovazquez.com

visit us at: www.eliovazquez.com

Cover Image: Top, own original design;
(Bottom-Bull) Adobe Stock Licensed Image.

ISBN-9798326865830
Publisher: Independently Published on June 2024
Printed in the United States of America

CONTENTS

Introduction
- About the Author   09
- Introduction   13
- History and Origin of Candlestick Charting   15
- Brief Overview of Candlestick Charting   17
- Importance of Understanding Candlestick Patterns in Trading   19

Chapter I Basics of Candlestick Patterns
- 1.1 What are Candlestick Charts   21
- 1.2 Components of a Candlestick, Body, Shadows, and Wicks   23
- 1.3 Reading Candlestick Patterns   25

Chapter II Single Candlestick Patterns
- 2.1 Doji   28
- 2.2 Hammer   30
- 2.3 Hanging Man   32
- 2.4 Shooting Star   34
- 2.5 Spinning Top   36
- 2.6 Marubozu   38

Chapter III Reversal Patterns
- 3.1 Engulfing Bullish Pattern   40
- 3.2 Engulfing Bearish Pattern   42
- 3.3 Piercing Pattern   44
- 3.4 Dark Cloud Cover   46
- 3.5 Morning Star   49
- 3.6 Evening Star   52
- 3.7 Three White Soldiers   55
- 3.8 Three Black Crows   57

Chapter III Reversal Patterns (Continuation)
3.9 Three Inside Up Pattern	59
3.10 Three Inside Down Pattern	62

Chapter IV Continuation Patterns
4.1 Bullish Flags	65
4.2 Bearish Flags	67
4.3 Bullish Pennants	70
4.4 Bearish Pennants	72
4.5 Rising Three Methods	74
4.6 Falling Three Methods	76

Chapter V Advance Candlestick Patterns
5.1 Tweezer Tops and Bottoms	78
5.2 Inside Bar	80
5.3 Outside Bar	82
5.4 Harami	84
5.5 Kicker Pattern	86
5.6 Abandoned Baby	88

Chapter VI Trading Strategies with Candlestick Patterns
6.1 Swing Trading Strategies	90
6.2 Day Trading Strategies	92
6.3 Position Trading Strategies	94
6.4 Combining Candlestick Patterns with Technical Indicators	96

Chapter VII Risk Management and Psychological Aspects
7.1 Importance of Risk Management in Trading	98
7.2 Overcoming Emotional Biases	100
7.3 Setting Realistic Expectations	102

Chapter VIII Case Studies
8.1 Examples of Successful Trades Using Candlestick Patterns	104

Chapter IX Creating a Trading Plan
9.1 Steps to Develop a Personalized Trading Plan Incorporating Candlestick Patterns **106**

Chapter X Conclusion
10.1 Summary of Key Points **108**
10.2 Encouragement to Continue Learning and Practicing **110**

Appendix I Glossary of Terms
11.1 Explanation of Trading Terminology Used Throughout the book. **112**

Appendix II Legal Disclaimer
12.1 Author Legal Disclaimer **115**

About the Author

Greetings, fellow traders and enthusiasts of the financial markets. It is with great pleasure and excitement that I welcome you to "Mastering Candlestick Chart Patterns," authored by Elio Vazquez. In the pages that follow, I am thrilled to share with you my passion for technical analysis and my deep insights into the world of candlestick charting.

Born and raised amidst the lush landscapes of a coffee farm in Cuba, I embarked on a remarkable journey that would take me from the idyllic countryside to the heights of the aviation industry and the dynamic world of stock trading. From an early age, I displayed a keen intellect and an insatiable curiosity about the world beyond my rural surroundings.

After completing my education, this young man answered the call of duty and enlisted in the Cuban Air Force's, where I honed the skills as a flight engineer and embarked on numerous missions that would shape my future forever. I pursued further military education and training in Russia, expanding my knowledge and expertise in aviation through the mid of 1980s. However, a desire for freedom and opportunity led me to make the bold decision to defect to Northern Canada from Rusia in 1991, leaving behind the familiar comforts of home in pursuit of a brighter future.

In Canada, I embarked on a new chapter of my life, seizing every opportunity for growth and advancement. In 1997, I achieved my lifelong dream of becoming an airline pilot, and begin soaring through the skies and traversing all continents with skill and precision.

Throughout my career in aviation, I never lost sight of my passion for the stock exchange and financial markets. In my spare time, I delved into the intricacies of trading, studying market trends and refining my strategies with dedication and perseverance.

Eventually, I made the transition to full-time trading in the summer of 2022, after retiring from the airlines and leveraging my wealth of experience and expertise to navigate the complexities of the financial world with confidence and acumen.

Today, I resides in the vibrant community of South Florida, Miami area where I enjoy the warm weather and picturesque ocean landscapes with my loving wife and children. As a retired airline pilot and successful trader, I continue to embrace new challenges and opportunities, driven by a relentless pursuit of excellence and a passion for lifelong learning.

With "Mastering Candlestick Chart Patterns," I share a wealth of knowledge and insights gleaned from decades of experience in both the aviation industry and the financial markets. Through this book, I hope to inspire and empower readers to unlock their full potential and achieve greater success in their own trading endeavors.

For years, I have been immersed in the captivating realm of trading, constantly seeking to unravel its mysteries and uncover strategies that lead to consistent success. Along this journey, I have come to appreciate the profound significance of candlestick patterns—a timeless tool that has stood the test of time and continues to empower traders with invaluable insights into market dynamics.

In this book, drawing upon my extensive experience and research, I aim to demystify candlestick chart patterns and provide you with a comprehensive roadmap to mastering their intricacies. Whether you're a novice trader eager to learn the fundamentals or a seasoned professional looking to refine your skills, this book is crafted to meet you at your level and elevate your understanding to new heights.

Through a combination of theoretical foundations, practical examples, and real-world case studies, I strive to equip you with the knowledge and techniques necessary to interpret candlestick patterns with confidence and precision.

From basic formations to advanced strategies, each chapter is meticulously crafted to build upon the last, guiding you on a transformative journey from novice to expert.

But beyond mere technical analysis, I believe that successful trading is as much about mindset and discipline as it is about strategy. Throughout this book, I will emphasize the importance of cultivating a trader's mindset, managing risk effectively, and maintaining emotional balance in the face of market volatility.

As the author, it is my sincerest hope that "Mastering Candlestick Chart Patterns" serves not only as a guidebook for navigating the complexities of the financial markets but also as a source of inspiration and empowerment on your journey to trading mastery. I invite you to embark on this transformative odyssey with me, and together, let us unlock the secrets of candlestick charting and pave the way to greater trading success.

Warm regards,

Elio Vazquez

Introduction:

Welcome to "**Mastering Candlestick Chart Patterns**," your definitive guide to unlocking the secrets of one of the most powerful tools in technical analysis. In the dynamic world of trading, understanding candlestick patterns can be the difference between success and failure. Whether you're a seasoned trader or just starting your journey into the financial markets, this book is designed to equip you with the knowledge and skills needed to navigate the complexities of candlestick charts with confidence and precision.

Candlestick charts have been used for centuries by traders around the globe to analyze price movements and predict future market trends. Originating in Japan in the 17th century, these visual representations of price action offer a unique insight into market sentiment, allowing traders to interpret the psychology of buyers and sellers.

In this book, we will delve deep into the world of candlestick chart patterns, exploring their significance, interpretation, and application in real-world trading scenarios. From the basics of candlestick construction to advanced pattern recognition techniques, each chapter will build upon the last, providing you with a comprehensive understanding of how to leverage candlestick charts to your advantage.

But "Mastering Candlestick Chart Patterns" is about more than just memorizing a list of formations. It's about understanding the underlying principles driving price movements and learning to interpret the subtle nuances of market dynamics. Throughout this book, we will not only discuss individual candlestick patterns but also delve into the broader concepts of trend analysis, support and resistance, and risk management.

Whether you're looking to identify trend reversals, spot entry and exit points, or fine-tune your trading strategy, "Mastering Candlestick Chart Patterns" will serve as your indispensable companion on the path to trading mastery. Packed with practical examples, actionable insights, and expert tips, this book is designed to empower you to take your trading to the next level.

So, are you ready to unlock the secrets of candlestick chart patterns and revolutionize your trading approach? Let's dive in and embark on this transformative journey together.

History and Origin of Candlestick Charts:

The history and origin of candlestick charts can be traced back to Japan in the 17th century, where they were used to analyze the price of rice contracts on the Dojima Rice Exchange in Osaka. The creator of candlestick charting is often attributed to Munehisa Homma, a Japanese rice trader from Sakata, who is believed to have developed the early principles of candlestick analysis.

Homma's trading activities and observations led him to develop a method of visually representing price movements and market sentiment. He recognized the importance of understanding human psychology in trading and noticed recurring patterns in market behavior.

Candlestick charts, as we know them today, evolved from Homma's observations and were refined over centuries by subsequent generations of Japanese traders. The visual representation provided by candlestick charts helped traders make better decisions by identifying patterns that indicated potential market reversals, continuations, and indecision.

Candlestick charting remained relatively unknown in the Western world until the late 20th century when it was introduced to the broader financial community by Steve Nison, an American technical analyst. Nison studied Japanese candlestick techniques and published the book "Japanese Candlestick Charting Techniques" in 1991, which brought candlestick charting to Western traders' attention.

Since then, candlestick charting has become a widely used tool in technical analysis across global financial markets. Traders and analysts rely on candlestick patterns to understand market dynamics, gauge investor sentiment, and make informed trading decisions.

The popularity of candlestick charting continues to grow, with traders incorporating advanced techniques and strategies to enhance their analysis and trading performance. Its rich history and proven effectiveness in predicting market movements have solidified candlestick charting as a cornerstone of technical analysis.

Here's a Brief Overview of Candlestick Charting:

Candlestick charting is a popular method used by traders and analysts to visualize price movements in financial markets. It originated in Japan centuries ago and was later popularized in the Western world. Candlestick charts display price data for a specific period (such as a day, week, or month) using candlestick-shaped symbols.

Each candlestick represents four key pieces of information: the opening price, the closing price, the highest price reached during the period, and the lowest price reached during the period. The body of the candlestick represents the price range between the opening and closing prices, with different colors or shading used to indicate whether the closing price was higher or lower than the opening price.

Candlestick patterns are formed by the arrangement of multiple candlesticks on a chart. These patterns can provide valuable insights into market sentiment and potential price movements. Some common candlestick patterns include the doji, hammer, shooting star, engulfing patterns, and many more. Traders use these patterns to identify potential entry and exit points for trades, as well as to gauge the strength of market trends.

Candlestick charting is often used in conjunction with other technical analysis tools and indicators to make more informed trading decisions. It's important for traders to understand the significance of different candlestick patterns and to use them within the context of broader market conditions and trends.

Overall, candlestick charting is a versatile and powerful tool for analyzing financial markets, offering valuable insights into market dynamics and helping traders identify potential trading opportunities.

Unlike many other resources, this book not only teaches you the theory behind candlestick patterns but also focuses on practical applications. Each chapter is designed to build your knowledge step-by-step, ensuring that you gain a thorough understanding of how to read, interpret, and act upon the signals provided by candlestick charts.

Importance of Understanding Candlestick Patterns in Trade:

Understanding candlestick patterns is crucial for traders for several reasons.

1. **Market Sentiment Analysis**: Candlestick patterns provide valuable insights into market sentiment. By analyzing the patterns formed by candlesticks, traders can gauge whether buyers or sellers are in control of the market and anticipate potential changes in direction.

2. **Price Action Analysis**: Candlestick patterns reflect the price action of an asset over a specific period. Traders can interpret these patterns to understand how prices are behaving and make informed decisions based on the patterns' implications for future price movements.

3. **Identification of Trends and Reversals**: Candlestick patterns can help traders identify trends and potential trend reversals. Patterns like engulfing patterns and dojis can signal shifts in market direction, providing traders with opportunities to enter or exit positions at favorable prices.

4. **Entry and Exit Signals**: Many candlestick patterns serve as entry and exit signals for trades. Traders can use patterns such as hammers, shooting stars, and bullish or bearish engulfing patterns to time their entries and exit with greater precision.

5. **Confirmation of Technical Analysis**: Candlestick patterns can confirm signals generated by other technical analysis tools and indicators. When multiple indicators point to the same conclusion as a candlestick pattern, traders may have higher confidence in their trading decisions.

6. **Risk Management**: Understanding candlestick patterns can help traders manage risk more effectively. For example, identifying reversal patterns near key support or resistance levels can prompt traders to place stop-loss orders to limit potential losses.

7. **Psychological Insights**: Candlestick patterns reflect the collective psychology of market participants. Patterns such as dojis, which indicate indecision or a standoff between buyers and sellers, can provide insights into market dynamics and potential shifts in sentiment.

8. **Adaptability Across Markets and Timeframes**: Candlestick patterns can be applied to various financial markets and timeframes, making them versatile tools for traders across different asset classes and trading styles.

Overall, understanding of candlestick patterns empowers traders to make more informed and strategic trading decisions, enhancing their ability to capitalize on market opportunities while managing risk effectively.

Chapter 1.0 Basic of Candlestick Charting
Chapter 1.1
What are Candlestick Charts:

Candlestick charts are a type of financial chart used to visualize price movements in financial markets, such as stocks, forex, commodities, and cryptocurrencies. They are made up of individual candlestick-shaped symbols, each representing price data for a specific period, such as a day, week, or month.

Each candlestick on a chart represents four key pieces of information about price action during the chosen period:

Candlestick Chart

1. **Opening Price**: The price at which the asset opened for the period. This is represented by the bottom of the candle's body (or the bottom of the candlestick if there's no body, as in the case of a Doji) on a bullish trend. The opposite applies for a bearish trend, the price at which the asset opened for the period is at the top of the candle's body, and the closing will be at the bottom of the candlestick.

2. **Closing Price**: The price at which the asset closed for the period. This is represented by the top of the candle's body on a bullish trend and the bottom of the candle's body on a bearish trend.

3. **High Price**: The highest price reached by the asset during the period. This is represented by the top of the candle's upper shadow (also called the wick or the upper wick).

4. **Low Price**: The lowest price reached by the asset during the period. This is represented by the bottom of the candle's lower shadow (or the bottom of the candlestick if there's no shadow).

The **Body** of the candlestick represents the price range between the opening and closing prices. It is typically filled or colored differently to indicate whether the closing price was higher or lower than the opening price. For example:

- **If the closing price is higher than the opening price, the body is often filled or colored green to represent a bullish candle.**

- **If the closing price is lower than the opening price, the body is often filled or colored red to represent a bearish candle.**

Candlestick charts provide visual cues about market sentiment and price action, making them popular tools for technical analysis. Traders use candlestick patterns to identify trends, reversals, and potential entry and exit points for trades.

Candlestick charts offer a more detailed view of price movements compared to other types of charts, such as line charts or bar charts, making them valuable for traders seeking to understand market dynamics and make informed trading decisions.

Chapter 1.2
Components of a Candlestick Chart:

Candlestick charts consist of several components that provide valuable information about price movements during a specific period. Here are the key components of a candlestick chart:

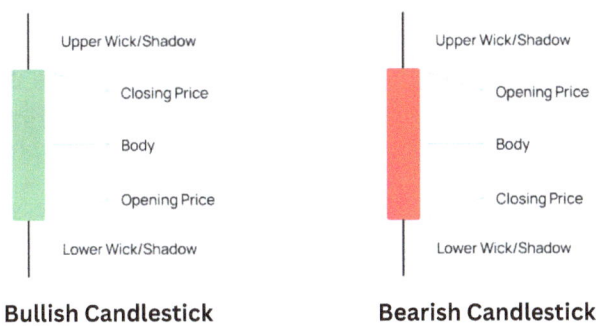

Candlestick Components

1. **Candlestick**: The main component of the chart is the candlestick itself, which represents the price action during a chosen period, such as a day, week, or month.

2. **Body**: The body of the candlestick represents the price range between the opening and closing prices for the period. It is typically filled or colored differently to indicate whether the closing price was higher or lower than the opening price.

3. **Wick or Shadow**: The wick, also known as the shadow, extends from the top and bottom of the candlestick body. It represents the highest and lowest prices reached during the period.

4. **Upper Wick**: The upper wick extends from the top of the body to the highest price reached during the period. It indicates the highest price at which the asset traded during that time frame.

5. **Lower Wick**: The lower wick extends from the bottom of the body to the lowest price reached during the period. It indicates the lowest price at which the asset is traded during that time frame.

6. **Open Price**: The open price is represented by the starting point of the candlestick body. It indicates the price at which the asset opened for the period.

7. **Close Price**: The close price is represented by the ending point of the candlestick body. It indicates the price at which the asset closed for the period.

8. **Color or Fill**: The color or fill of the candlestick body is used to indicate whether the closing price was higher or lower than the opening price. Different charting platforms may use different colors or fills, but common conventions include green or white for bullish (closing price higher than opening price) and red or black for bearish (closing price lower than opening price).

By analyzing these components, traders can gain insights into market sentiment, identify potential trends or reversals, and make informed decisions about entering or exiting trades. Candlestick charts provide a visual representation of price movements that is easy to interpret and widely used in technical analysis.

Chapter 1.3
Reading Candlestick Patterns:

Reading candlestick patterns involves interpreting the formations and combinations of candlesticks on a chart to gain insights into market sentiment and potential price movements. Here's a step-by-step guide to reading candlestick patterns effectively:

1. **Understand Basic Candlestick Anatomy**: Familiarize yourself with the basic components of a candlestick, including the body, wick (or shadow), upper wick, and lower wick. Each component provides valuable information about price action during a specific period.

2. **Recognize Individual Candlestick Patterns**: Learn to identify common individual candlestick patterns and understand their implications. Some basic patterns include:

- **Doji**: Represents indecision in the market, with opening and closing prices nearly equal.

- **Hammer**: Appears at the bottom of a downtrend and suggests a potential bullish reversal.

- **Shooting Star**: Appears at the top of an uptrend and suggests a potential bearish reversal.

- **Engulfing Patterns**: Bullish engulfing pattern occurs when a large bullish candlestick engulfs the previous smaller bearish candlestick, indicating a potential bullish reversal. Bearish engulfing pattern is the opposite.

3. **Study Pattern Combinations**: Pay attention to combinations of multiple candlesticks forming patterns that provide stronger signals. For example:

- **Three Inside Up**: A bullish reversal pattern consisting of three candlesticks where the second and third candles are engulfed by the first candle.

- **Three Black Crows**: A bearish reversal pattern consisting of three consecutive long red (or black) candlesticks, signaling a potential downtrend continuation.

4. **Consider Market Context**: Assess the broader market context, including trends, support and resistance levels, and volume, to validate candlestick signals. For example:

- A bullish reversal pattern is more reliable when it occurs near a support level in an uptrend.

- Confirmation from increasing volume can strengthen the validity of a candlestick pattern signal.

5. **Use Candlestick Patterns in Combination with Other Indicators**: Combine candlestick patterns with other technical indicators, such as moving averages, RSI (Relative Strength Index), or MACD (Moving Average Convergence Divergence), to confirm signals and enhance trading decisions.

6. **Practice and Gain Experience**: Continuously practice identifying and interpreting candlestick patterns on historical charts and real-time market data. Over time, you'll develop a better intuition for recognizing patterns and their significance.

Remember that while candlestick patterns can provide valuable insights, they are not foolproof indicators and should be used in conjunction with other forms of analysis and risk management techniques.

Chapter 2.0 Single Candlestick Patterns
Chapter 2.1
Doji Candlestick Patterns:

Doji candlestick patterns are significant formations that indicate indecision in the market. They occur when the opening and closing prices of an asset are very close or nearly equal, resulting in a small or nonexistent body and long wicks. Doji patterns suggest a standoff between buyers and sellers, where neither group has gained control over the price action during the period. Here are some key points about Doji candlestick patterns:

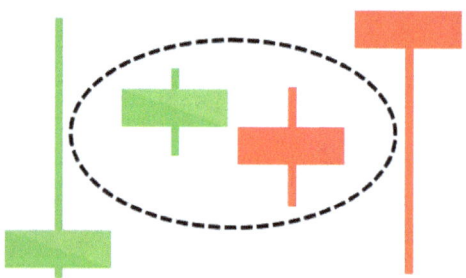

Doji Candlestick Pattern

1. **Appearance**: A Doji candlestick typically has a small or nonexistent body, with opening and closing prices that are close together. The length of the wicks can vary, but they are often relatively long compared to the body.

2. **Types of Doji**:

- **Classic Doji**: The opening and closing prices are virtually the same, resulting in a very small or nonexistent body.
- **Long-legged Doji**: The wicks on both ends of the candlestick are longer, indicating greater price volatility during the period.
- **Dragonfly Doji**: The opening and closing prices are at the high of the period, with a long lower wick. It suggests a potential bullish reversal.

- **Gravestone Doji**: The opening and closing prices are at the low of the period, with a long upper wick. It suggests a potential bearish reversal.

3. **Significance**: Doji patterns reflect market indecision and suggest a potential reversal or continuation depending on their context:
- In an uptrend, a Doji may signal a potential reversal to a downtrend, especially if it appears after a series of bullish candlesticks.
- In a downtrend, a Doji may signal a potential reversal to an uptrend, especially if it appears after a series of bearish candlesticks.
- In a sideways or ranging market, a Doji may indicate a continuation of the consolidation phase.

4. **Confirmation**: Traders often look for confirmation from other technical indicators or candlestick patterns to validate the significance of a Doji pattern. For example, increased volume or a subsequent candlestick confirming the reversal can strengthen the signal.

5. **Caution**: While Doji patterns can provide valuable insights into market sentiment, they should not be relied upon as standalone indicators. It's essential to consider other factors, such as trend analysis, support and resistance levels, and volume when making trading decisions based on Doji patterns.

Understanding and recognizing Doji candlestick patterns can help traders identify potential reversal or continuation opportunities in the market, but it's crucial to use them in conjunction with other forms of analysis for more robust trading decisions.

Chapter 2.2
Hammer Candlestick Patterns:

The Hammer candlestick pattern is a significant formation that often signals a potential reversal in the market. It typically appears at the bottom of a downtrend and suggests that selling pressure may be exhausted, with buyers starting to regain control. Here are some key points about Hammer candlestick patterns:

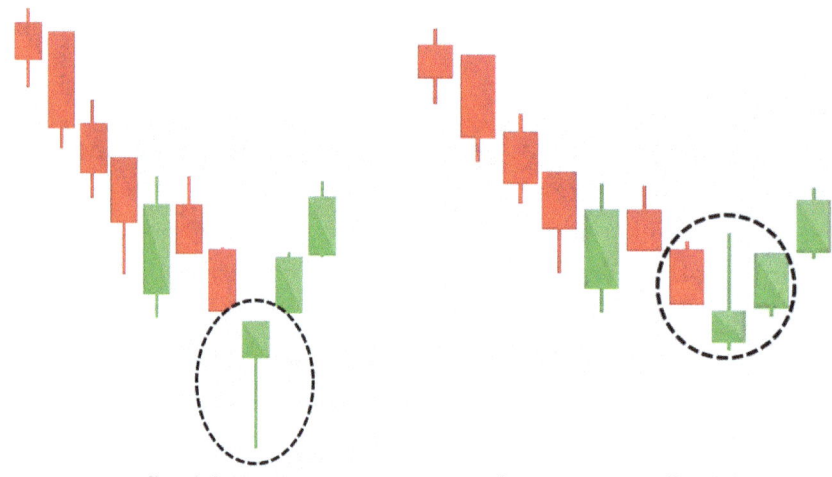

Hammer Candlestick Pattern   **Inverted Hammer Candlestick Pattern**

1. **Appearance**: A Hammer candlestick has a small body near the top of the candlestick range, with a long lower wick (shadow) that is at least two times the length of the body. There may or may not be an upper wick. The body is typically bullish, meaning the closing price is higher than the opening price, but it can also be neutral.

2. **Characteristics:**

- The long lower wick indicates that prices fell significantly during the period but were later rejected, with buyers stepping in to push prices back up toward the opening level or higher.
- The small body near the top of the candlestick range suggests that buyers were able to regain control by the end of the period, despite the initial selling pressure.

3. **Significance**:

- The Hammer pattern is considered a bullish reversal signal when it appears at the end of a downtrend, indicating that sellers may be exhausted and that a potential reversal to an uptrend may occur.
- It suggests that buyers have started to outnumber sellers, leading to a shift in market sentiment from bearish to bullish.
- The longer the lower wick relative to the body, the more significant the pattern is considered.

4. **Confirmation**: Traders often look for confirmation from other factors to validate the significance of a Hammer pattern:
- Increased volume during the formation of the Hammer can strengthen the signal.
- A subsequent bullish candlestick confirming the reversal can provide further confirmation.
- The presence of other technical indicators, such as support levels or bullish divergence in oscillators, can also support the bullish reversal thesis.

5. **Caution**: While the Hammer pattern can provide valuable insights into potential trend reversals, it should not be relied upon as a standalone indicator. It's essential to consider other factors, such as overall market conditions, trend analysis, and volume, when making trading decisions based on Hammer patterns.

Recognizing and understanding Hammer candlestick patterns can help traders identify potential buying opportunities at the bottom of downtrends, but it's crucial to use them in conjunction with other forms of analysis for more robust trading decisions.

Chapter 2.3
Hanging Man Candlestick Pattern:

The Hanging Man candlestick pattern is a significant formation that often signals a potential reversal in the market. It typically appears at the top of an uptrend and suggests that selling pressure may be starting to outweigh buying pressure, potentially indicating a reversal to a downtrend. Here are some key points about Hanging Man candlestick patterns:

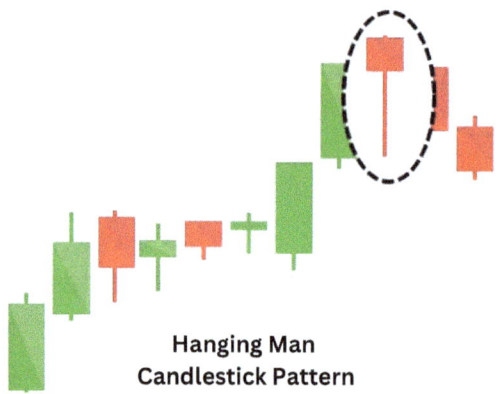

Hanging Man
Candlestick Pattern

1. **Appearance**: A Hanging Man candlestick has a small body near the top of the candlestick range, with a long lower wick (shadow) that is at least two times the length of the body. There may or may not be an upper wick. The body is typically bearish, meaning the closing price is lower than the opening price, but it can also be neutral.

2. **Characteristics**:
- The long lower wick indicates that prices fell significantly during the period but were later rejected, with buyers stepping in to push prices back up toward the opening level or higher.
- The small body near the top of the candlestick range suggests that buyers were unable to maintain control by the end of the period, despite the initial buying pressure.

3. **Significance**:

- The Hanging Man pattern is considered a bearish reversal signal when it appears at the end of an uptrend, indicating that buyers may be exhausted and that a potential reversal to a downtrend may occur.
- It suggests that sellers have started to outnumber buyers, leading to a shift in market sentiment from bullish to bearish.
- The longer the lower wick relative to the body, the more significant the pattern is considered.

4. **Confirmation**: Traders often look for confirmation from other factors to validate the significance of a Hanging Man pattern:
- Increased volume during the formation of the Hanging Man can strengthen the signal.
- A subsequent bearish candlestick confirming the reversal can provide further confirmation.
- The presence of other technical indicators, such as resistance levels or bearish divergence in oscillators, can also support the bearish reversal thesis.

5. **Caution**: While the Hanging Man pattern can provide valuable insights into potential trend reversals, it should not be relied upon as a standalone indicator. It's essential to consider other factors, such as overall market conditions, trend analysis, and volume, when making trading decisions based on Hanging Man patterns.

Recognizing and understanding Hanging Man candlestick patterns can help traders identify potential selling opportunities at the top of uptrends, but it's crucial to use them in conjunction with other forms of analysis for more robust trading decisions.

Chapter 2.4
Shooting Star Candlestick Pattern:

The Shooting Star candlestick pattern is a significant formation that often signals a potential reversal in the market. It typically appears at the top of an uptrend and suggests that selling pressure may be starting to outweigh buying pressure, potentially indicating a reversal to a downtrend. Here are some key points about Shooting Star candlestick patterns:

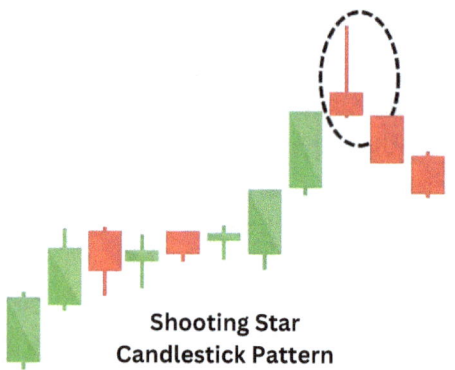

Shooting Star
Candlestick Pattern

1. **Appearance**:

A Shooting Star candlestick has a small body near the bottom of the candlestick range, with a long upper wick (shadow) that is at least two times the length of the body. There may or may not be a lower wick. The body is typically bearish, meaning the closing price is lower than the opening price, but it can also be neutral.

2. **Characteristics**:

- The long upper wick indicates that prices rose significantly during the period but were later rejected, with sellers stepping in to push prices back down toward the opening level or lower.

- The small body near the bottom of the candlestick range suggests that buyers were unable to maintain control by the end of the period, despite the initial buying pressure.

3. **Significance**:

- The Shooting Star pattern is considered a bearish reversal signal when it appears at the end of an uptrend, indicating that buyers may be exhausted and that a potential reversal to a downtrend may occur.

- It suggests that sellers have started to outnumber buyers, leading to a shift in market sentiment from bullish to bearish.
- The longer the upper wick relative to the body, the more significant the pattern is considered.

4. **Confirmation**: Traders often look for confirmation from other factors to validate the significance of a Shooting Star pattern:
   - Increased volume during the formation of the Shooting Star can strengthen the signal.
   - A subsequent bearish candlestick confirming the reversal can provide further confirmation.
   - The presence of other technical indicators, such as resistance levels or bearish divergence in oscillators, can also support the bearish reversal thesis.

5. **Caution**: While the Shooting Star pattern can provide valuable insights into potential trend reversals, it should not be relied upon as a standalone indicator. It's essential to consider other factors, such as overall market conditions, trend analysis, and volume, when making trading decisions based on Shooting Star patterns.

Recognizing and understanding Shooting Star candlestick patterns can help traders identify potential selling opportunities at the top of uptrends, but it's crucial to use them in conjunction with other forms of analysis for more robust trading decisions.

Chapter 2.5
Spinning Top Candlestick Pattern:

The Spinning Top candlestick pattern is a significant formation that indicates indecision in the market. It typically appears when there is a tug-of-war between buyers and sellers, resulting in a small body near the middle of the candlestick range and long upper and lower wicks. Here are some key points about the Spinning Top candlestick pattern:

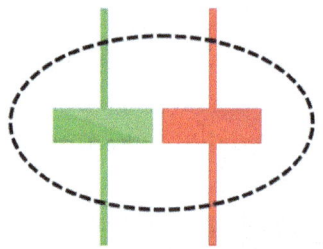

Spinning Top Candlesticks

1. **Appearance**: A Spinning Top candlestick has a small body near the middle of the candlestick range, with long upper and lower wicks (shadows) of roughly equal length. The body can be bullish, bearish, or neutral, and its size relative to the wicks may vary.

2. **Characteristics**:
- The small body near the middle of the candlestick range indicates that the opening and closing prices are close together, suggesting indecision between buyers and sellers.
- The long upper and lower wicks indicate that prices moved significantly in both directions during the period, with neither buyers nor sellers able to establish control.

3. **Significance**:

- The Spinning Top pattern suggests a temporary pause or consolidation in the market, with neither bulls nor bears able to gain the upper hand.
- It indicates uncertainty and indecision among market participants, often occurring during periods of market transition or before a significant price move.
- While the Spinning Top itself does not provide a clear directional bias, it can serve as a warning sign of potential volatility or a reversal depending on its context.

4. **Confirmation**: Traders often look for confirmation from other factors to validate the significance of a Spinning Top pattern:
- Increased volume during the formation of the Spinning Top can signal potential follow-through and continuation of the indecision.
- Subsequent candlestick patterns or price action confirming a breakout or reversal can provide further confirmation.

5. **Caution**: While the Spinning Top pattern can provide valuable insights into market indecision, it should not be relied upon as a standalone indicator. It's essential to consider other factors, such as overall market conditions, trend analysis, and volume when making trading decisions based on Spinning Top patterns.

Recognizing and understanding Spinning Top candlestick patterns can help traders identify potential periods of indecision and volatility in the market, but it's crucial to use them in conjunction with other forms of analysis for more robust trading decisions.

Chapter 2.6
Marubozu Candlestick Pattern:

The Marubozu candlestick pattern is a significant formation characterized by a candlestick with little to no wicks and a long body, indicating strong buying or selling pressure throughout the trading period. Here are some key points about the Marubozu candlestick pattern:

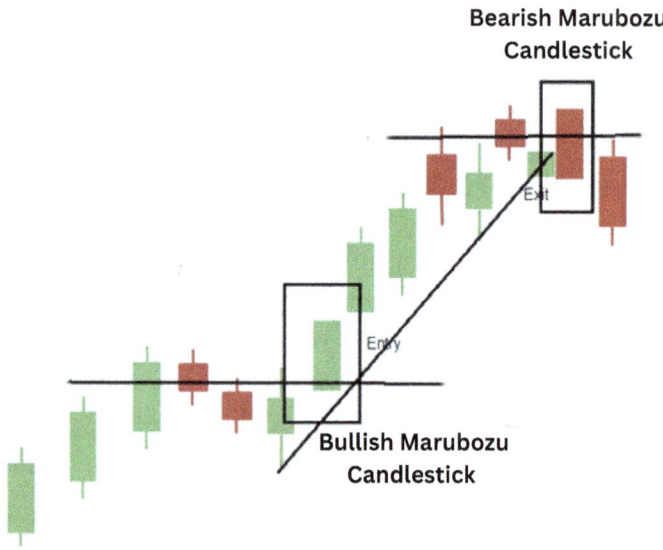

1. **Appearance**: A Marubozu candlestick has a long body with little to no wicks (shadows) on either end. The opening or closing price is typically at one extreme of the candlestick range, with no significant price movement during the period.

2. **Characteristics**:

   - **Bullish Marubozu**: The candlestick has a long body with no upper or lower wick, indicating that prices opened at the low of the period and closed at the high. It suggests strong buying pressure throughout the trading session.

   - **Bearish Marubozu**: The candlestick has a long body with no upper or lower wick, indicating that prices opened at the high of the period and closed at the low. It suggests strong selling pressure throughout the trading session.

3. **Significance**:

- The Marubozu pattern signifies a decisive and one-sided market sentiment, with buyers or sellers dominating the entire trading period.
- In the case of a Bullish Marubozu, it suggests strong bullish momentum and a potential continuation of the uptrend.
- In the case of a Bearish Marubozu, it suggests strong bearish momentum and a potential continuation of the downtrend.

4. **Confirmation**: Traders often look for confirmation from other factors to validate the significance of a Marubozu pattern:
- Increased volume during the formation of the Marubozu can strengthen the signal.
- Confirmation from other technical indicators or price action can provide further validation of the directional bias.

5. **Caution**: While the Marubozu pattern can provide valuable insights into strong market sentiment, it should not be relied upon as a standalone indicator. It's essential to consider other factors, such as overall market conditions, trend analysis, and volume, when making trading decisions based on Marubozu patterns.

Recognizing and understanding Marubozu candlestick patterns can help traders identify potential trends and gauge market sentiment, but it's crucial to use them in conjunction with other forms of analysis for more robust trading decisions.

Chapter 3.0 Reversal Patterns
Chapter 3.1
Engulfing Bullish Candlestick Pattern:

The Engulfing Bullish Candlestick Pattern is a potent formation in technical analysis, indicative of a potential reversal from a downtrend to an uptrend. This pattern consists of two candlesticks, where the second candlestick body completely engulfs the body of the preceding candlestick. Here's a comprehensive overview of this bullish reversal pattern:

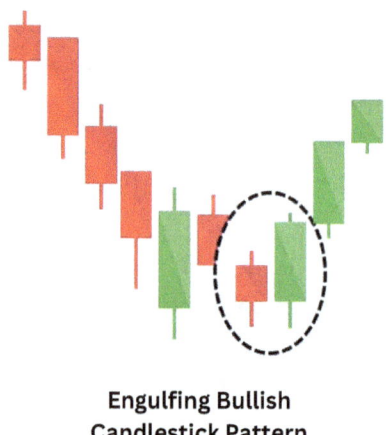

Engulfing Bullish Candlestick Pattern

1. **Formation**: The Engulfing Bullish Candlestick Pattern typically occurs after a downtrend, signaling a shift in market sentiment from bearish to bullish. The first candlestick is usually a smaller bearish candlestick, followed by a larger bullish candlestick that completely engulfs the body of the preceding candlestick.

2. **Characteristics**:
- The first candlestick in the pattern reflects the prevailing downtrend, with sellers dominating the market and pushing prices lower.
- The second candlestick opens lower than the previous candlestick close but rallies strongly throughout the period, closing higher than the previous candlestick open.

- The body of the second candlestick engulfs the entire body of the first candlestick, indicating a decisive shift in momentum from bearish to bullish.

3. **Significance**:
- The Engulfing Bullish Candlestick Pattern is considered a strong bullish reversal signal, suggesting that buyers have overwhelmed sellers and are likely to continue driving prices higher.
 - It signifies a potential turning point in the market, with the potential for an uptrend to develop following the pattern's formation.
 - The larger the second candlestick relative to the first, the more significant the pattern is considered, as it indicates a more forceful reversal.

4. **Confirmation**: While the Engulfing Bullish Candlestick Pattern is compelling on its own, confirmation from other factors strengthens the signal:
- Increased trading volume during the formation of the pattern can validate the strength of the bullish reversal.
- Confirmation from other technical indicators, such as moving averages or momentum oscillators, can provide additional confirmation of the uptrend reversal.

5. **Caution**: Despite its reliability, traders should exercise caution and consider other factors before making trading decisions based solely on the Engulfing Bullish Candlestick Pattern. Market context, overall trend analysis, and risk management should all be taken into account to ensure well-informed trading decisions.

In conclusion, the Engulfing Bullish Candlestick Pattern is a formidable tool in the arsenal of technical analysts, providing clear signals of potential trend reversals. However, like all technical patterns, it should be used in conjunction with other forms of analysis to confirm its validity and maximize trading success.

Chapter 3.2
Engulfing Bearish Candlestick Pattern:

The Engulfing Bearish Candlestick Pattern is a significant formation in technical analysis, indicating a potential reversal from an uptrend to a downtrend. This pattern consists of two candlesticks, where the second candlestick body completely engulfs the body of the preceding candlestick, signaling a shift in market sentiment from bullish to bearish. Here's a detailed overview of this bearish reversal pattern:

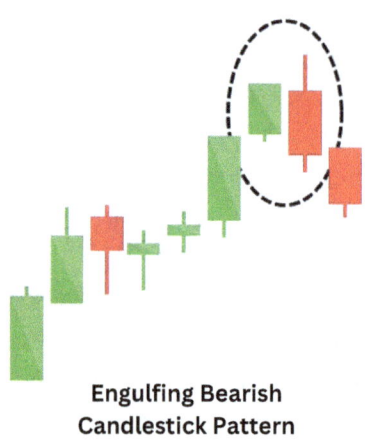

Engulfing Bearish Candlestick Pattern

1. **Formation**: The Engulfing Bearish Candlestick Pattern typically occurs after an uptrend, suggesting a change in market sentiment from bullish to bearish. The first candlestick is usually a smaller bullish candlestick, followed by a larger bearish candlestick that completely engulfs the body of the preceding candlestick.

2. **Characteristics**:
- The first candlestick in the pattern reflects the prevailing uptrend, with buyers dominating the market and pushing prices higher.
- The second candlestick opens higher than the previous candlestick close but declines strongly throughout the period, closing lower than the previous candlestick open.

- The body of the second candlestick engulfs the entire body of the first candlestick, indicating a decisive shift in momentum from bullish to bearish.

3. **Significance**:
- The Engulfing Bearish Candlestick Pattern is considered a strong bearish reversal signal, suggesting that sellers have overwhelmed buyers and are likely to continue driving prices lower.
- It signifies a potential turning point in the market, with the potential for a downtrend to develop following the pattern's formation.
- The larger the second candlestick relative to the first, the more significant the pattern is considered, as it indicates a more forceful reversal.

4. **Confirmation**: While the Engulfing Bearish Candlestick Pattern is powerful on its own, confirmation from other factors strengthens the signal:
- Increased trading volume during the formation of the pattern can validate the strength of the bearish reversal.
- Confirmation from other technical indicators, such as moving averages or momentum oscillators, can provide additional confirmation of the downtrend reversal.

5. **Caution**: Despite its reliability, traders should exercise caution and consider other factors before making trading decisions solely based on the Engulfing Bearish Candlestick Pattern. Market context, overall trend analysis, and risk management should all be taken into account to ensure well-informed trading decisions.

In summary, the Engulfing Bearish Candlestick Pattern is a potent tool for identifying potential trend reversals, providing clear signals of a shift in market sentiment from bullish to bearish. However, like all technical patterns, it should be used in conjunction with other forms of analysis for confirmation and risk management purposes.

Chapter 3.3
Piercing Candlestick Pattern:

The Piercing Candlestick Pattern is a bullish reversal pattern in technical analysis that typically occurs at the end of a downtrend. It consists of two candlesticks, where the first candlestick is a bearish candlestick and the second candlestick is a bullish candlestick that "pierces" through the body of the first candlestick, closing above its midpoint. Here's a detailed overview of this pattern:

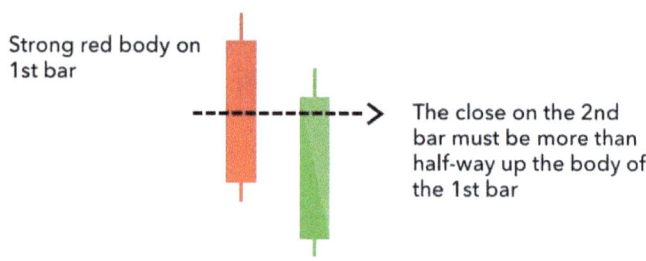

Piercing Candlestick Pattern

1. **Formation**: The Piercing Candlestick Pattern usually emerges after a prolonged downtrend, indicating potential exhaustion of selling pressure and a possible reversal in market sentiment. The first candlestick is typically a bearish candlestick with a strong downward movement, followed by a bullish candlestick that opens below the previous candle's low and closes above its midpoint.

2. **Characteristics**:
- The first candlestick in the pattern reflects the prevailing downtrend, with sellers dominating the market and pushing prices lower.
- The second candlestick opens lower than the previous candle's low, indicating a continuation of the downtrend initially.

- However, buyers step in during the trading period, driving prices higher and causing the second candlestick to close above the midpoint of the first candlestick body.
- The bullish candlestick "pierces" through the body of the previous bearish candlestick, signaling potential bullish momentum and a shift in market sentiment.

3. **Significance**:
- The Piercing Candlestick Pattern is considered a strong bullish reversal signal, suggesting that buyers have overwhelmed sellers and are likely to continue driving prices higher.
- It signifies a potential turning point in the market, with the potential for an uptrend to develop following the pattern's formation.
- The stronger the bullish candlestick and the deeper it penetrates the body of the previous bearish candlestick, the more significant the pattern is considered.

4. **Confirmation**: While the Piercing Candlestick Pattern is robust on its own, confirmation from other factors strengthens the signal:
   - Increased trading volume during the formation of the pattern can validate the strength of the bullish reversal.
   - Confirmation from other technical indicators, such as moving averages or momentum oscillators, can provide additional confirmation of the uptrend reversal.

5. **Caution**: Despite its reliability, traders should exercise caution and consider other factors before making trading decisions solely based on the Piercing Candlestick Pattern. Market context, overall trend analysis, and risk management should all be taken into account to ensure well-informed trading decisions.

In summary, the Piercing Candlestick Pattern is a potent tool for identifying potential trend reversals, providing clear signals of a shift in market sentiment from bearish to bullish. However, like all technical patterns, it should be used in conjunction with other forms of analysis for confirmation and risk management purposes.

Chapter 3.4
Dark Cloud Cover Candlestick Pattern:

The Dark Cloud Cover candlestick pattern is a significant formation in technical analysis that typically occurs at the end of an uptrend, signaling a potential reversal to a downtrend. This pattern consists of two candlesticks, where the first candlestick is a bullish candlestick and the second candlestick is a bearish candlestick that opens above the previous candle's high but closes below its midpoint. Here's a detailed overview of this bearish reversal pattern:

Dark Cloud Cover
Candlestick Pattern

1. **Formation**: The Dark Cloud Cover pattern often emerges after a prolonged uptrend, suggesting potential exhaustion of buying pressure and a possible shift in market sentiment from bullish to bearish. The first candlestick is typically a bullish candlestick with a strong upward movement, followed by a bearish candlestick that opens above the previous candle's high and closes below its midpoint.

2. **Characteristics**:
- The first candlestick in the pattern reflects the prevailing uptrend, with buyers dominating the market and pushing prices higher.

- The second candlestick opens higher than the previous candle's high, indicating a continuation of the uptrend initially.
- However, sellers' step in during the trading period, driving prices lower and causing the second candlestick to close below the midpoint of the previous bullish candlestick body.
- The bearish candlestick "clouds" the optimism of the previous bullish candlestick, signaling potential bearish momentum and a shift in market sentiment.

3. **Significance**:
- The Dark Cloud Cover pattern is considered a strong bearish reversal signal, suggesting that sellers have overwhelmed buyers and are likely to continue driving prices lower.
- It signifies a potential turning point in the market, with the potential for a downtrend to develop following the pattern's formation.
- The stronger the bearish candlestick and the deeper it penetrates the body of the previous bullish candlestick, the more significant the pattern is considered.

4. **Confirmation**: While the Dark Cloud Cover pattern is robust on its own, confirmation from other factors strengthens the signal:
- Increased trading volume during the formation of the pattern can validate the strength of the bearish reversal.
- Confirmation from other technical indicators, such as moving averages or momentum oscillators, can provide additional confirmation of the downtrend reversal.

5. **Caution**: Despite its reliability, traders should exercise caution and consider other factors before making trading decisions solely based on the Dark Cloud Cover pattern. Market context, overall trend analysis, and risk management should all be taken into account to ensure well-informed trading decisions.

In summary, the Dark Cloud Cover pattern is a potent tool for identifying potential trend reversals, providing clear signals of a shift in market sentiment from bullish to bearish. However, like all technical patterns, it should be used in conjunction with other forms of analysis for confirmation and risk management purposes.

Chapter 3.5
Morning Star Candlestick Pattern:

The Morning Star candlestick pattern is a significant formation in technical analysis that typically occurs at the end of a downtrend, signaling a potential reversal to an uptrend. This pattern consists of three candlesticks, usually appearing as follows:

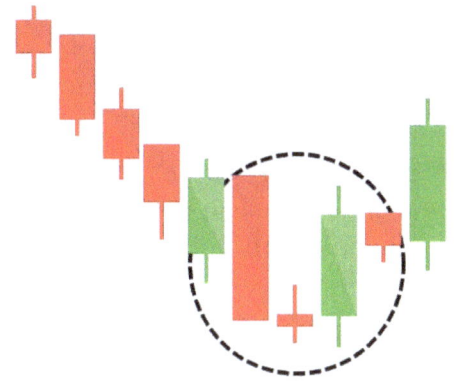

Morning Star Candlestick Pattern

1. **First Candlestick (Bearish)**: The first candlestick is a long bearish candlestick, indicating a strong downward movement in prices. This candlestick confirms the prevailing downtrend.
2. **Second Candlestick (Indecisive)**: The second candlestick is a smaller-bodied candlestick, often referred to as a doji or a spinning top, characterized by its small body with long upper and lower wicks. This candlestick reflects market indecision and suggests a potential pause or hesitation in the downtrend.

3. **Third Candlestick (Bullish)**: The third candlestick is a long bullish candlestick that closes above the midpoint of the first candlestick body. This bullish candlestick confirms the reversal and signals the potential beginning of an uptrend.

Here's a detailed overview of the Morning Star candlestick pattern:

1. **Formation**: The Morning Star pattern typically emerges after a prolonged downtrend, indicating potential exhaustion of selling pressure and a possible shift in market sentiment from bearish to bullish.

2. **Characteristics**:
- The first candlestick in the pattern reflects the prevailing downtrend, with sellers dominating the market and pushing prices lower.
- The second candlestick indicates market indecision, with neither buyers no sellers able to establish control, resulting in a smaller-bodied candlestick with long wicks.
- The third candlestick is a bullish candlestick that opens below the previous candle close but rallies strongly throughout the period, closing above the midpoint of the first candlestick body. This bullish candlestick confirms the reversal and signals potential bullish momentum.

3. **Significance**:
- The Morning Star pattern is considered a strong bullish reversal signal, suggesting that buyers have overwhelmed sellers and are likely to continue driving prices higher.
- It signifies a potential turning point in the market, with the potential for an uptrend to develop following the pattern's formation.
- The stronger the bullish candlestick and the higher it closes relative to the first candlestick body, the more significant the pattern is considered.

4. **Confirmation**: While the Morning Star pattern is robust on its own, confirmation from other factors strengthens the signal:
- Increased trading volume during the formation of the pattern can validate the strength of the bullish reversal.
- Confirmation from other technical indicators, such as moving averages or momentum oscillators, can provide additional confirmation of the uptrend reversal.

5. **Caution**: Despite its reliability, traders should exercise caution and consider other factors before making trading decisions solely based on the Morning Star pattern. Market context, overall trend analysis, and risk management should all be taken into account to ensure well-informed trading decisions.

Morning Star Candlestick Pattern

In summary, the Morning Star pattern is a potent tool for identifying potential trend reversals, providing clear signals of a shift in market sentiment from bearish to bullish. However, like all technical patterns, it should be used in conjunction with other forms of analysis for confirmation and risk management purposes.

Chapter 3.6
Evening Star Candlestick Pattern:

The Evening Star candlestick pattern is a significant formation in technical analysis that typically occurs at the end of an uptrend, signaling a potential reversal to a downtrend. This pattern consists of three candlesticks, usually appearing as follows:

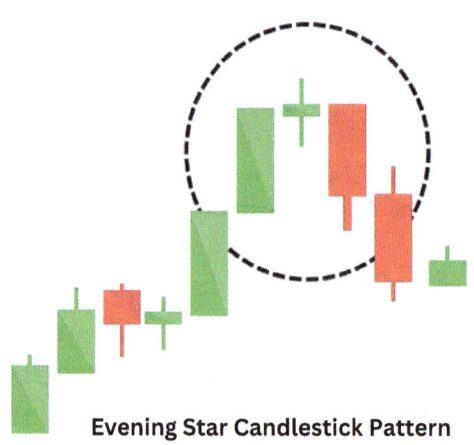

Evening Star Candlestick Pattern

1. **Formation**: The Evening Star pattern typically emerges after a prolonged uptrend, indicating potential exhaustion of buying pressure and a possible shift in market sentiment from bullish to bearish.

Here's a detailed overview of the Evening Star candlestick pattern:

- **First Candlestick (Bullish)**: The first candlestick is a long bullish candlestick, indicating a strong upward movement in prices. This candlestick confirms the prevailing uptrend.

- **Second Candlestick (Indecisive)**: The second candlestick is a smaller-bodied candlestick, often referred to as a doji or a spinning top, characterized by its small body with long upper and lower wicks. This candlestick reflects market indecision and suggests a potential pause or hesitation in the uptrend.

- **Third Candlestick (Bearish)**: The third candlestick is a long bearish candlestick that closes below the midpoint of the first candlestick's body. This bearish candlestick confirms the reversal and signals the potential beginning of a downtrend.

2. **Characteristics**:
- The first candlestick in the pattern reflects the prevailing uptrend, with buyers dominating the market and pushing prices higher.
- The second candlestick indicates market indecision, with neither buyers no sellers able to establish control, resulting in a smaller-bodied candlestick with long wicks.
- The third candlestick is a bearish candlestick that opens above the previous candle close but declines strongly throughout the period, closing below the midpoint of the first candlestick body. This bearish candlestick confirms the reversal and signals potential bearish momentum.

3. **Significance**:
- The Evening Star pattern is considered a strong bearish reversal signal, suggesting that sellers have overwhelmed buyers and are likely to continue driving prices lower.
- It signifies a potential turning point in the market, with the potential for a downtrend to develop following the pattern formation.
- The stronger the bearish candlestick and the lower it closes relative to the first candlestick body, the more significant the pattern is considered.

4. **Confirmation**: While the Evening Star pattern is robust on its own, confirmation from other factors strengthens the signal:
- Increased trading volume during the formation of the pattern can validate the strength of the bearish reversal.
- Confirmation from other technical indicators, such as moving averages or momentum oscillators, can provide additional confirmation of the downtrend reversal.

5. **Caution**: Despite its reliability, traders should exercise caution and consider other factors before making trading decisions solely based on the Evening Star pattern. Market context, overall trend analysis, and risk management should all be taken into account to ensure well-informed trading decisions.

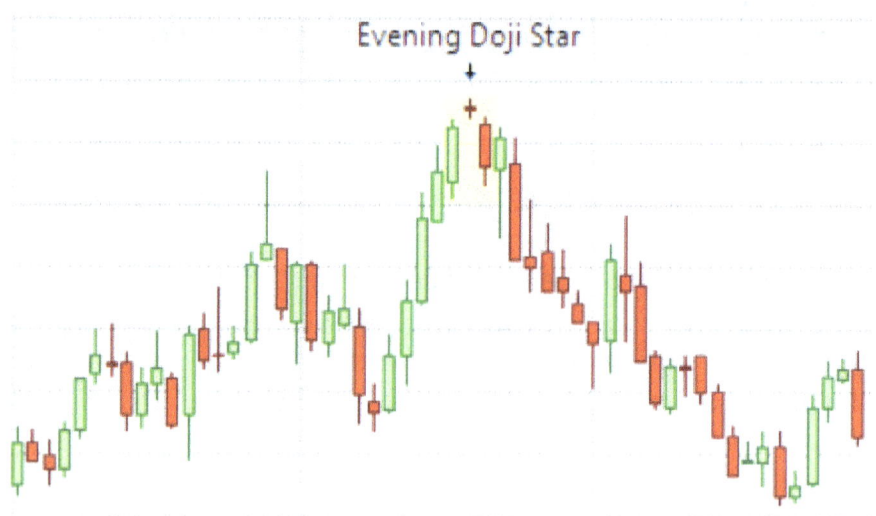

Evening Star Candlestick Pattern

In summary, the Evening Star pattern is a potent tool for identifying potential trend reversals, providing clear signals of a shift in market sentiment from bullish to bearish. However, like all technical patterns, it should be used in conjunction with other forms of analysis for confirmation and risk management purposes.

Chapter 3.7
Three White Soldiers Candlestick Pattern:

The Three White Soldiers candlestick pattern is a strong bullish reversal pattern that typically occurs at the end of a downtrend. It consists of three consecutive bullish candlesticks, each with higher closes than the previous one, signaling a shift in market sentiment from bearish to bullish. Here's a detailed overview of this pattern:

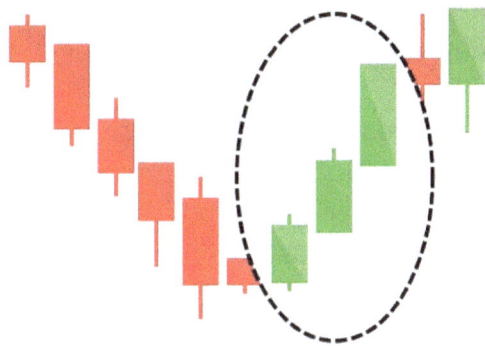

Three White Soldiers Candlestick Pattern

1. **Formation**: The Three White Soldiers pattern usually emerges after a prolonged downtrend, indicating the potential exhaustion of selling pressure and a possible reversal in market sentiment.

2. **Characteristics**:
- Each candlestick in the pattern is a long bullish candlestick with little to no upper wick and closing near its high, reflecting strong buying pressure throughout the trading period.
- Each successive candlestick opens higher than the previous one and closes higher than its opening price, indicating a steady increase in buying momentum.
- The pattern demonstrates a clear and decisive shift from bearishness to bullishness, with buyers taking control of the market and pushing prices higher.

3. **Significance**:
- The Three White Soldiers pattern is considered one of the strongest bullish reversal signals, suggesting a high probability of a trend reversal from downtrend to uptrend.
- It signifies a potential turning point in the market, with the potential for a sustained uptrend to develop following the pattern's formation.
- The stronger and more uniform the three bullish candlesticks are, the more significant the pattern is considered.

4. **Confirmation**: While the Three White Soldiers pattern is robust on its own, confirmation from other factors strengthens the signal:
- Increased trading volume during the formation of the pattern can validate the strength of the bullish reversal.
- Confirmation from other technical indicators, such as moving averages or momentum oscillators, can provide additional confirmation of the uptrend reversal.

5. **Caution**: Despite its reliability, traders should exercise caution and consider other factors before making trading decisions solely based on the Three White Soldiers pattern. Market context, overall trend analysis, and risk management should all be taken into account to ensure well-informed trading decisions.

In summary, the Three White Soldiers pattern is a potent tool for identifying potential trend reversals, providing clear signals of a shift in market sentiment from bearish to bullish. However, like all technical patterns, it should be used in conjunction with other forms of analysis for confirmation and risk management purposes.

Chapter 3.8
Three Black Crows Candlestick Pattern:

The "Three Black Crows" candlestick pattern is a significant bearish reversal pattern that typically forms at the end of an uptrend. It consists of three consecutive long bearish candlesticks, each closing near its low and opening within the body of the previous candlestick. Here's a detailed overview:

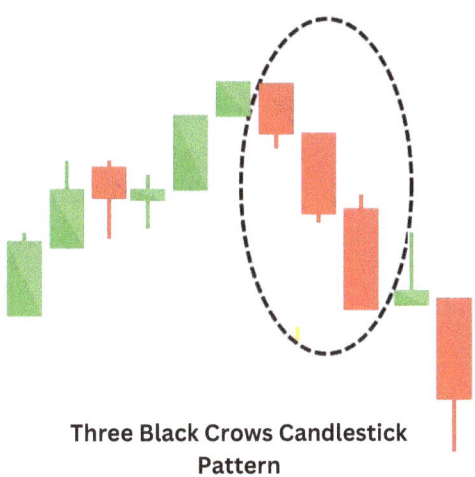

Three Black Crows Candlestick Pattern

1. **Formation**: The Three Black Crows pattern often emerges after an extended uptrend, signaling potential exhaustion of buying pressure and a possible shift in market sentiment from bullish to bearish.

2. **Characteristics**:
- Each candlestick in the pattern is a long bearish candlestick with little to no lower wick and closing near its low, indicating strong selling pressure throughout the trading period.
- Each successive candlestick opens within the body of the previous one and closes lower than its opening price, demonstrating a continuation of the bearish momentum.
- The pattern reflects a clear and decisive shift from bullishness to bearishness, with sellers taking control of the market and pushing prices lower.

3. **Significance**:
- The Three Black Crows pattern is considered one of the strongest bearish reversal signals, suggesting a high probability of a trend reversal from uptrend to downtrend.
- It signifies a potential turning point in the market, with the potential for a sustained downtrend to develop following the pattern formation.
- The stronger and more uniform the three bearish candlesticks are, the more significant the pattern is considered.

4. **Confirmation**: While the Three Black Crows pattern is potent on its own, confirmation from other factors strengthens the signal:
- Increased trading volume during the formation of the pattern can validate the strength of the bearish reversal.
- Confirmation from other technical indicators, such as moving averages or momentum oscillators, can provide additional confirmation of the downtrend reversal.

5. **Caution**: Despite its reliability, traders should exercise caution and consider other factors before making trading decisions solely based on the Three Black Crows pattern. Market context, overall trend analysis, and risk management should all be taken into account to ensure well-informed trading decisions.

In summary, the Three Black Crows pattern is a potent tool for identifying potential trend reversals, providing clear signals of a shift in market sentiment from bullish to bearish. However, like all technical patterns, it should be used in conjunction with other forms of analysis for confirmation and risk management purposes.

Chapter 3.9
Three Inside Up Candlestick Pattern:

The Three Inside Up candlestick pattern is a bullish reversal pattern that typically forms at the end of a downtrend, signaling a potential reversal to an uptrend. This pattern consists of three candlesticks and is considered a confirmation of the trend reversal. Here's a detailed breakdown of the Three Inside Up candlestick pattern:

Three Inside Up Candlestick Pattern

1. **Formation**: The Three Inside Up candlestick pattern is a bullish reversal pattern consisting of three specific candlesticks that signal a potential change in trend direction from bearish to bullish. Here's a detailed explanation of its formation and characteristics.

2. **Characteristics:**
- **First Candle**: The first candle is a long bearish (red or black) candlestick, indicating the continuation of the downtrend and strong selling pressure.

- **Second Candle**: The second candle is a small bullish (green or white) candlestick that forms within the body of the first candle. It represents indecision and the weakening of the downward momentum. This candlestick is often referred to as an "inside bar" because it is contained within the high and low range of the previous bearish candle.

- **Third Candle**: The third candle is a bullish (green or white) candlestick that closes above the high of the first bearish candle, confirming the reversal. This candle indicates a shift in market sentiment from bearish to bullish and suggests the potential start of an uptrend.

3. **Significance**:
- The Three Inside Up pattern signals that the bears are losing control and the bulls are gaining strength.
- The small bullish candle within the first bearish candle indicates indecision, and the final bullish candle closing above the first candle's high confirms the bullish reversal.
- This pattern suggests that traders may look for buying opportunities as the trend changes direction.

4. **Confirmation**: Initial Three Inside Up Pattern Formation.
- First Candle: A long bearish candle, indicating continued selling pressure.
- Second Candle: A small bullish candle that forms within the body of the first candle, showing a pause in the downtrend.
- Third Candle: A bullish candle that closes above the opening price of the first candle, suggesting a potential reversal.

5.**Caution**: While the Three Inside Up candlestick pattern can be a powerful tool in predicting bullish reversals, traders should use caution and confirm the pattern with additional technical indicators, volume analysis, and broader market context. Proper risk management and multi-timeframe analysis are crucial to avoid false signals and enhance the reliability of this pattern in trading decisions.

By understanding the formation and implications of the Three Inside Up candlestick pattern, traders can better identify potential reversal points and make more informed trading decisions.

In summary, confirmation is crucial when trading the Three Inside Up candlestick pattern to enhance the reliability of the bullish reversal signal. By combining the pattern with other technical indicators, volume analysis, and key support levels, traders can make more informed and confident trading decisions, ultimately improving their chances of success in the markets.

Chapter 3.10
Three Inside Down Candlestick Pattern:

The Three Inside Down candlestick pattern is a bearish reversal pattern that typically appears at the end of an uptrend, signaling a potential shift to a downtrend. This pattern consists of three specific candlesticks and is considered to be a strong indicator of a reversal when identified correctly. Here is a detailed breakdown of the Three Inside Down candlestick pattern:

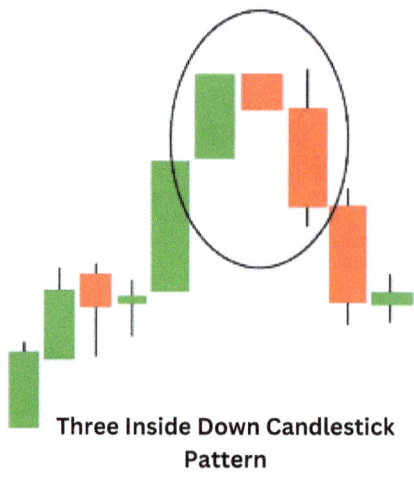
Three Inside Down Candlestick Pattern

1. **Formation**: The Three Inside Down candlestick pattern is a bearish reversal pattern that signals a potential shift from an uptrend to a downtrend. This pattern consists of three candlesticks and is a strong indicator of a reversal when identified correctly. Here's a detailed breakdown of its formation.

1. **Characteristics**:
- **First Candle**: The first candlestick in the pattern is a long bullish (green or white) candle. This candle reflects strong buying pressure and confirms the prevailing uptrend.

- **Second Candle**: A smaller bearish candle within the body of the first candle. The second candlestick is a smaller bearish (red or black) candle. This candle opens and closes within the body of the first bullish candle, indicating a potential pause in buying pressure and the emergence of selling interest. This candle is often referred to as an "inside bar" because it is contained within the range of the previous candle.

- **Third Candle**: A bearish candle closing below the first candles open. The third candlestick is a bearish (red or black) candle. It opens lower than the second candle's close and closes below the opening price of the first bullish candle. This candle confirms the reversal by closing below the low of the first bullish candle, signaling that sellers have taken control.

3. **Significance**:
- Early Reversal Signal: The pattern signals a potential shift from an uptrend to a downtrend. This early indication allows traders to position themselves accordingly, potentially entering short positions or exiting long positions before a significant downtrend begins.

- Confirmation of Bearish Sentiment: The pattern consists of three candles that collectively confirm a change in market sentiment from bullish to bearish. The first bullish candle reflects the prevailing uptrend, the second smaller bearish candle suggests hesitation among buyers, and the third bearish candle confirms that sellers have gained control.

- Reliability: The Three Inside Down pattern is considered reliable when confirmed with other technical analysis tools. Its formation often marks a meaningful shift in momentum, making it a valuable tool in a trader's arsenal.

- Volume Analysis: Increased volume on the third candle can add significance to the pattern. Higher volume indicates stronger conviction among sellers, making the reversal signal more robust.

- Support and Resistance: The pattern often forms near resistance levels, adding to its reliability. If the pattern appears at or near a significant resistance level, it can strengthen the bearish reversal signal.

4. **Confirmation**:
- First Candle: The stock forms a long bullish candle, continuing the uptrend.

- Second Candle: The next day, the stock opens lower and forms a small bearish candle within the body of the first candle, indicating a potential pause and uncertainty.

- Third Candle: On the third day, the stock opens lower and closes below the opening price of the first bullish candle, confirming a bearish reversal.

In this scenario, the pattern's significance lies in its ability to alert traders to a potential reversal before a major downtrend begins. By recognizing this pattern, traders can prepare to short the stock, close long positions, or adjust their trading strategies to mitigate risk.

5. **Caution**: While the Three Inside Down candlestick pattern can be a powerful tool in predicting bearish reversals, it's essential to use caution and confirm the pattern with additional technical indicators, volume analysis, and broader market context. Proper risk management and multi-timeframe analysis are crucial to avoid false signals and enhance the reliability of this pattern in trading decisions.

In summary, the Three Inside Down candlestick pattern is a significant tool for traders, offering a reliable signal of a potential bearish reversal in an uptrend. By understanding its formation, significance, and how to confirm the pattern with additional analysis, traders can make more informed decisions, manage risk effectively, and capitalize on market reversals.

Chapter 4.0 Continuation Patterns
Chapter 4.1
Bullish Flag Candlestick Patterns:

Bullish Flag patterns are significant continuation patterns often seen in technical analysis, indicating a brief pause in an uptrend before the price resumes its upward movement. They are characterized by a sharp, upward price movement (flagpole), followed by a consolidation period (flag) that typically slopes against the prevailing trend. Here's a detailed overview of Bullish Flag patterns:

Bullish Flag Candlestick Pattern

1. **Formation**: Bullish Flag patterns typically occur after a strong upward price movement, representing a temporary consolidation or correction phase within the context of an ongoing uptrend. The flagpole is formed by the initial sharp price increase, while the flag portion is characterized by a series of lower highs and higher lows, creating a visual resemblance to a flag on a flagpole.

2. **Characteristics**:
- **Flagpole**: The flagpole is the initial sharp upward movement in price that precedes the flag formation. It's usually a strong and swift price increase driven by significant buying pressure.
- **Flag**: The flag portion of the pattern is a period of consolidation or correction, typically marked by lower highs and higher lows. The consolidation phase often takes the form of a rectangular or parallelogram pattern sloping against the prevailing trend.

- **Volume**: Volume tends to decline during the formation of the flag pattern, reflecting decreased trading activity and market participation compared to the flagpole.

3. **Significance**:
- Bullish Flag patterns are considered continuation patterns, signaling a temporary pause or consolidation within an ongoing uptrend before the price resumes its upward movement.
- The pattern suggests that buyers are taking a breather after the initial rally, allowing the market to digest gains and build momentum for the next leg higher.
- Bullish Flag patterns are typically seen as bullish signals, indicating a high probability of the uptrend continuing once the price breaks out above the upper boundary of the flag pattern.

4. **Confirmation**: Confirmation of a Bullish Flag pattern can be sought through:
- **Breakout**: A decisive breakout above the upper boundary of the flag pattern on increased volume confirms the bullish continuation bias.
- **Price Targets**: The projected price target of a Bullish Flag pattern is often estimated by measuring the height of the flagpole and adding it to the breakout point.

5. **Caution**: While Bullish Flag patterns are reliable continuation signals, traders should exercise caution and consider other factors such as overall market conditions, trend strength, and potential support and resistance levels before making trading decisions solely based on the pattern.

In summary, Bullish Flag patterns are valuable tools for identifying opportunities to participate in the continuation of uptrends. By understanding the structure and significance of these patterns, traders can enhance their ability to identify favorable entry points and manage risk effectively.

Chapter 4.2
Bearish Flag Candlestick Patterns:

Bearish Flag patterns are significant continuation patterns in technical analysis, indicating a brief pause in a downtrend before the price resumes its downward movement. These patterns are characterized by a sharp, downward price movement (flagpole), followed by a consolidation period (flag) that typically slopes against the prevailing trend. Here's a detailed overview of Bearish Flag patterns:

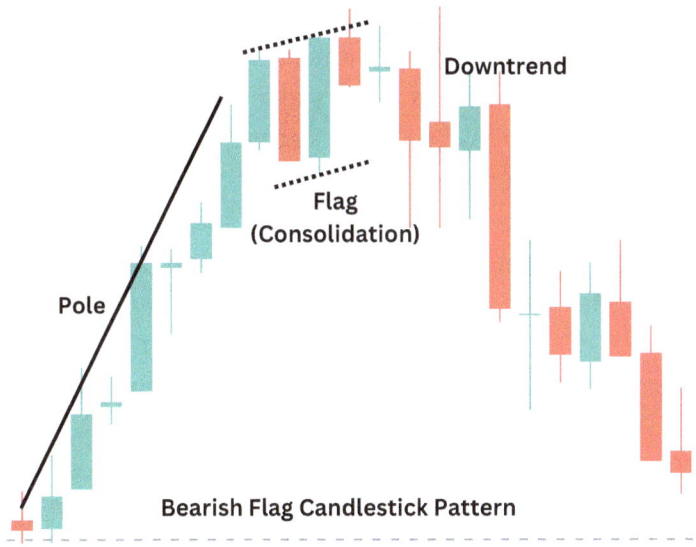

Bearish Flag Candlestick Pattern

1. **Formation**: Bearish Flag patterns typically occur after a strong downward price movement, representing a temporary consolidation or correction phase within the context of an ongoing downtrend. The flagpole is formed by the initial sharp price decrease, while the flag portion is characterized by a series of higher lows and lower highs, creating a visual resemblance to a flag on a flagpole.

2. **Characteristics**:
- **Flagpole**: The flagpole is the initial sharp downward movement in price that precedes the flag formation. It's usually a strong and swift price decrease driven by significant selling pressure.

- **Flag**: The flag portion of the pattern is a period of consolidation or correction, typically marked by higher lows and lower highs. The consolidation phase often takes the form of a rectangular or parallelogram pattern sloping against the prevailing trend.
- **Volume**: Volume tends to decline during the formation of the flag pattern, reflecting decreased trading activity and market participation compared to the flagpole.

3. **Significance**:
- Bearish Flag patterns are considered continuation patterns, signaling a temporary pause or consolidation within an ongoing downtrend before the price resumes its downward movement.
- The pattern suggests that sellers are taking a breather after the initial decline, allowing the market to consolidate losses and gather momentum for the next leg lower.
- Bearish Flag patterns are typically seen as bearish signals, indicating a high probability of the downtrend continuing once the price breaks out below the lower boundary of the flag pattern.

4. **Confirmation**: Confirmation of a Bearish Flag pattern can be sought through:
- **Breakout**: A decisive breakout below the lower boundary of the flag pattern on increased volume confirms the bearish continuation bias.
- **Price Targets**: The projected price target of a Bearish Flag pattern is often estimated by measuring the height of the flagpole and subtracting it from the breakout point.

5. **Caution**: While Bearish Flag patterns are reliable continuation signals, traders should exercise caution and consider other factors such as overall market conditions, trend strength, and potential support and resistance levels before making trading decisions solely based on the pattern.

In summary, Bearish Flag patterns are valuable tools for identifying opportunities to participate in the continuation of downtrends. By understanding the structure and significance of these patterns, traders can enhance their ability to identify favorable entry points and manage risk effectively.

Chapter 4.3
Bullish Pennant Candlestick Patterns:

Bullish Pennant patterns are significant continuation patterns in technical analysis, indicating a brief consolidation or pause in an uptrend before the price resumes its upward movement. These patterns are characterized by a sharp, upward price movement (flagpole), followed by a symmetrical triangle-shaped consolidation (pennant) with converging trendlines. Here's a detailed overview of Bullish Pennant patterns:

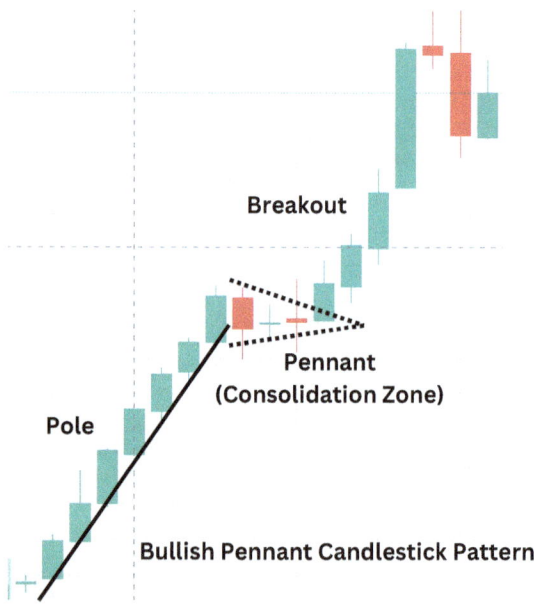

1. **Formation**: Bullish Pennant patterns typically occur after a strong upward price movement, representing a temporary consolidation or correction phase within the context of an ongoing uptrend. The flagpole is formed by the initial sharp price increase, while the pennant portion is characterized by converging trend lines forming a symmetrical triangle pattern.

2. **Characteristics**:
- **Flagpole**: The flagpole is the initial sharp upward movement in price that precedes the pennant formation. It's usually a strong and swift price increase driven by significant buying pressure.

- **Pennant**: The pennant portion of the pattern is a period of consolidation or correction, typically marked by converging trend lines forming a symmetrical triangle pattern. This consolidation phase represents a temporary pause in the uptrend as buyers and sellers reach equilibrium.
- **Volume**: Volume tends to decline during the formation of the pennant pattern, reflecting decreased trading activity and market participation compared to the flagpole.

3. **Significance**:
- Bullish Pennant patterns are considered continuation patterns, signaling a temporary pause or consolidation within an ongoing uptrend before the price resumes its upward movement.
- The pattern suggests that buyers are taking a breather after the initial rally, allowing the market to consolidate gains and build momentum for the next leg higher.
- Bullish Pennant patterns are typically seen as bullish signals, indicating a high probability of the uptrend continuing once the price breaks out above the upper boundary of the pennant pattern.

4. **Confirmation**: Confirmation of a Bullish Pennant pattern can be sought through:
- **Breakout**: A decisive breakout above the upper boundary of the pennant pattern on increased volume confirms the bullish continuation bias.
- **Price Targets**: The projected price target of a Bullish Pennant pattern is often estimated by measuring the height of the flagpole and adding it to the breakout point.

5. **Caution**: While Bullish Pennant patterns are reliable continuation signals, traders should exercise caution and consider other factors such as overall market conditions, trend strength, and potential support and resistance levels before making trading decisions solely based on the pattern.

In summary, Bullish Pennant patterns are valuable tools for identifying opportunities to participate in the continuation of uptrends. By understanding the structure and significance of these patterns, traders can enhance their ability to identify favorable entry points and manage risk effectively.

Chapter 4.4
Bearish Pennant Candlestick Patterns:

Bearish Pennant patterns are significant continuation patterns in technical analysis, indicating a brief consolidation or pause in a downtrend before the price resumes its downward movement. These patterns are characterized by a sharp, downward price movement (flagpole), followed by a symmetrical triangle-shaped consolidation (pennant) with converging trendlines. Here's a detailed overview of Bearish Pennant patterns:

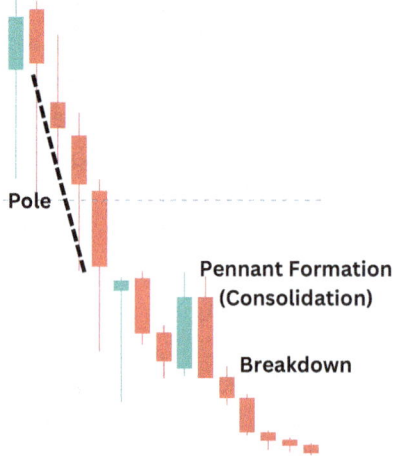

1. **Formation**: Bearish Pennant patterns typically occur after a strong downward price movement, representing a temporary consolidation or correction phase within the context of an ongoing downtrend. The flagpole is formed by the initial sharp price decrease, while the pennant portion is characterized by converging trend lines forming a symmetrical triangle pattern.

2. **Characteristics**:

- **Flagpole**: The flagpole is the initial sharp downward movement in price that precedes the pennant formation. It's usually a strong and swift price decrease driven by significant selling pressure.

- **Pennant**: The pennant portion of the pattern is a period of consolidation or correction, typically marked by converging trend lines forming a symmetrical triangle pattern.

This consolidation phase represents a temporary pause in the downtrend as buyers and sellers reach equilibrium.
- **Volume**: Volume tends to decline during the formation of the pennant pattern, reflecting decreased trading activity and market participation compared to the flagpole.

3. **Significance**:
- Bearish Pennant patterns are considered continuation patterns, signaling a temporary pause or consolidation within an ongoing downtrend before the price resumes its downward movement.
- The pattern suggests that sellers are taking a breather after the initial decline, allowing the market to consolidate losses and gather momentum for the next leg lower.
- Bearish Pennant patterns are typically seen as bearish signals, indicating a high probability of the downtrend continuing once the price breaks out below the lower boundary of the pennant pattern.

4. **Confirmation**: Confirmation of a Bearish Pennant pattern can be sought through:
- **Breakout**: A decisive breakout below the lower boundary of the pennant pattern on increased volume confirms the bearish continuation bias.
- **Price Targets**: The projected price target of a Bearish Pennant pattern is often estimated by measuring the height of the flagpole and subtracting it from the breakout point.

5. **Caution**: While Bearish Pennant patterns are reliable continuation signals, traders should exercise caution and consider other factors such as overall market conditions, trend strength, and potential support and resistance levels before making trading decisions solely based on the pattern.

In summary, Bearish Pennant patterns are valuable tools for identifying opportunities to participate in the continuation of downtrends. By understanding the structure and significance of these patterns, traders can enhance their ability to identify favorable entry points and manage risk effectively.

Chapter 4.5
Rising Three Methods Candlestick Pattern:

The Rising Three Methods is a bullish candlestick pattern that occurs during a downtrend. It's characterized by a series of three small-bodied candlesticks (either bullish or bearish) sandwiched between a long bullish candlestick and another bullish candlestick. Here's how it typically forms:

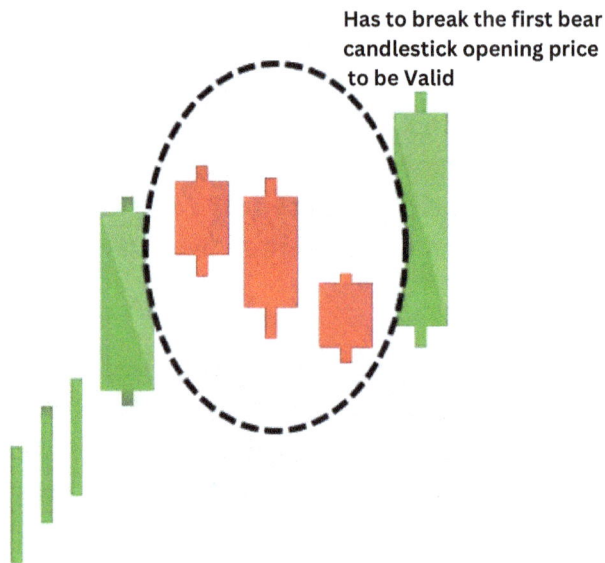

Rising Three Methods Candlestick Pattern

1. **First Candlestick (Long Bullish)**: The pattern starts with a long bullish candlestick, indicating strong buying pressure and potentially signaling the beginning of a bullish trend reversal.

2. **Second, Third, and Fourth Candlesticks (Small-bodied)**: Following the long bullish candlestick, three small-bodied candlesticks may be either bullish or bearish. These candlesticks represent a period of consolidation or minor retracement within the overall downtrend.

3. **Fifth Candlestick (Long Bullish)**: The pattern concludes with another long bullish candlestick, which typically closes above the close of the first candlestick. This reaffirms the bullish sentiment and suggests that buyers have regained control of the market.

Here's what the Rising Three Methods pattern signifies:

- **Bullish Reversal**: The Rising Three Methods pattern suggests a potential reversal of a downtrend, with the long bullish candlesticks signaling increased buying pressure and a shift in market sentiment.

- **Consolidation**: The small-bodied candlesticks in the middle of the pattern represent a period of consolidation or indecision, during which the market retraces slightly before resuming its upward movement.

- **Confirmation**: Traders often seek confirmation of the pattern through subsequent price action, such as further bullish candlesticks or a break above resistance levels.

- **Volume**: It's also essential to consider volume trends during the formation of the pattern. Ideally, increasing volume during the bullish candlesticks reinforces the bullish reversal signal.

While the Rising Three Methods pattern can be a reliable bullish reversal signal, traders should exercise caution and consider other factors, such as overall market conditions, trend strength, and potential support and resistance levels, before making trading decisions solely based on the pattern. Additionally, using additional technical indicators or chart patterns can help confirm the validity of the pattern and improve trading decisions.

Chapter 4.6
Falling Three Methods Candlestick Pattern:

The Falling Three Methods is a bearish candlestick pattern that occurs during an uptrend. It's characterized by a series of three small-bodied candlesticks (either bullish or bearish) sandwiched between a long bearish candlestick and another bearish candlestick. Here's how it typically forms:

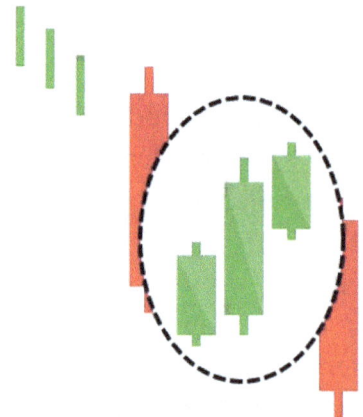

Falling Three Methods Candlestick Pattern

1. **First Candlestick (Long Bearish)**: The pattern starts with a long bearish candlestick, indicating strong selling pressure and potentially signaling the beginning of a bearish trend reversal.

2. **Second, Third, and Fourth Candlesticks (Small-bodied)**: Following the long bearish candlestick, three small-bodied candlesticks may be either bullish or bearish. These candlesticks represent a period of consolidation or minor retracement within the overall uptrend.

3. **Fifth Candlestick (Long Bearish)**: The pattern concludes with another long bearish candlestick, which typically closes below the close of the first candlestick. This reaffirms the bearish sentiment and suggests that sellers have regained control of the market.

Here's what the Falling Three Methods pattern signifies:

- **Bearish Reversal**: The Falling Three Methods pattern suggests a potential reversal of an uptrend, with the long bearish candlesticks signaling increased selling pressure and a shift in market sentiment.

- **Consolidation**: The small-bodied candlesticks in the middle of the pattern represent a period of consolidation or indecision, during which the market retraces slightly before resuming its downward movement.

- **Confirmation**: Traders often seek confirmation of the pattern through subsequent price action, such as further bearish candlesticks or a break below support levels.

- **Volume**: It's also essential to consider volume trends during the formation of the pattern. Ideally, increasing volume during the bearish candlesticks reinforces the bearish reversal signal.

While the Falling Three Methods pattern can be a reliable bearish reversal signal, traders should exercise caution and consider other factors, such as overall market conditions, trend strength, and potential support and resistance levels, before making trading decisions solely based on the pattern. Additionally, using additional technical indicators or chart patterns can help confirm the validity of the pattern and improve trading decisions.

Chapter 5.0 Advanced Candlestick Patterns
Chapter 5.1
Tweezer Tops and Bottoms Candlestick Patterns:

The Tweezer Tops and Bottoms are significant reversal patterns in technical analysis, signaling potential changes in market direction. They consist of two or more candlesticks with identical highs (Tweezer Tops) or lows (Tweezer Bottoms). Here's a detailed overview of both patterns:

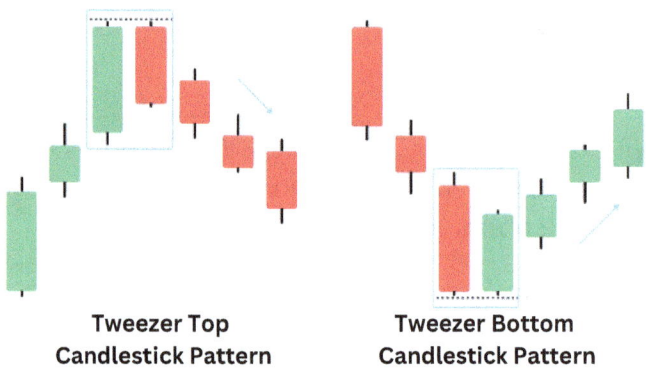

Tweezer Top Candlestick Pattern   Tweezer Bottom Candlestick Pattern

1. **Tweezer Tops**:

- **Formation**: Tweezer Tops occur at the peak of an uptrend and consist of two candlesticks with identical highs, indicating that the market reached a resistance level and failed to move higher.
- **Characteristics**:
- The first candlestick is typically bullish and part of the ongoing uptrend.
- The second candlestick is bearish and forms immediately after the first candle, with its height matching the height of the previous candle.

- **Significance**:
- Tweezer Tops suggest that buyers attempted to push the price higher but failed, indicating potential exhaustion of buying pressure and a possible trend reversal.

- They are often seen as a bearish reversal signal, especially when confirmed by other technical indicators or price action signals.
- Traders may look for additional confirmation, such as a bearish engulfing pattern or a break below support levels, to validate the reversal signal.

2. Tweezer Bottoms:

- **Formation**: Tweezer Bottoms occur at the bottom of a downtrend and consist of two candlesticks with identical lows, indicating that the market reached a support level and failed to move lower.

- **Characteristics**:
- The first candlestick is typically bearish and part of the ongoing downtrend.
- The second candlestick is bullish and forms immediately after the first candle, with its low matching the low of the previous candle.

- **Significance**:
- Tweezer Bottoms suggests that sellers attempted to push the price lower but failed, indicating potential exhaustion of selling pressure and a possible trend reversal.
- They are often seen as a bullish reversal signal, especially when confirmed by other technical indicators or price action signals.
- Traders may look for additional confirmation, such as a bullish engulfing pattern or a break above resistance levels, to validate the reversal signal.

In summary, Tweezer Tops and Bottoms are valuable tools for identifying potential trend reversals, providing clear signals of market indecision and potential exhaustion of buying or selling pressure. However, like all technical patterns, they should be used in conjunction with other forms of analysis for confirmation and risk management purposes.

Chapter 5.2
Inside Bar Candlestick Patterns:

Inside Bar candlestick patterns are significant price action patterns that indicate a potential consolidation or continuation in the market. This pattern consists of two candlesticks, where the second candlestick is completely contained within the range of the previous candlestick. Here's a detailed overview:

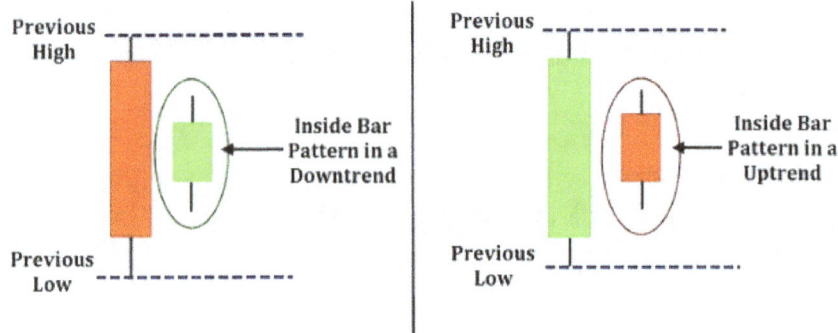

Inside Bar Candlestick Pattern

1. **Formation**:
- Inside Bar patterns occur when the range (high to low) of the second candlestick is completely contained within the range of the first candlestick. This means that the high and low of the second candlestick are within the high and low of the first candlestick.
- The first candlestick is referred to as the "mother bar" or "outside bar," and the second candlestick is the "inside bar."

2. **Characteristics**:
- The first candlestick is typically larger and has a wider range compared to the second candlestick.
- The second candlestick has a smaller range and is completely engulfed by the high and low of the first candlestick.
- Inside Bars can occur in both uptrends and downtrends.

3. **Significance**:
- Inside Bar patterns suggest a period of consolidation or indecision in the market, where buyers and sellers are in equilibrium.
- They indicate a potential pause in the prevailing trend, with traders waiting for more clarity or a catalyst before committing to new positions.
- Inside Bars can also signify a continuation of the existing trend if they occur within a strong trend.

4. **Trading Strategies**:

- **Breakout Trading**: Traders often look for a breakout of the high or low of the Inside Bar to signal potential continuation or reversal. A breakout above the high of the Inside Bar in an uptrend or below the low in a downtrend could signal a continuation of the trend.
- **Range Trading**: Some traders choose to trade Inside Bars within the range of the mother bar, buying near the low and selling near the high of the Inside Bar.

5. **Confirmation**:
- Traders may seek confirmation of Inside Bar patterns through other technical indicators or price action signals, such as volume analysis, trend lines, or support and resistance levels.

In summary, Inside Bar patterns are valuable tools for identifying potential consolidation or continuation in the market. While they can provide clear signals of indecision or a pause in the trend, traders should always consider other factors and use additional confirmation before making trading decisions based solely on Inside Bars.

Chapter 5.3
Outside Bar Candlestick Patterns:

Outside Bar candlestick patterns, also known as "engulfing" patterns, are significant price action patterns that indicate a potential reversal in the market. This pattern consists of two candlesticks, where the second candlestick completely engulfs the range of the first candlestick, thus overshadowing it. Here's a detailed overview:

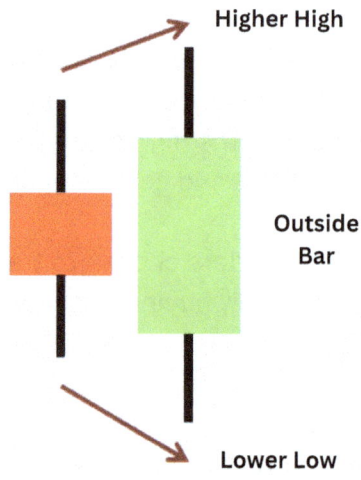

Outside Bar Candlestick Pattern

1. **Formation:**
- Outside Bar patterns occur when the range (high to low) of the second candlestick completely engulfs the range of the first candlestick. This means that the high of the second candlestick is higher than the high of the first candlestick, and the low of the second candlestick is lower than the low of the first candlestick.

- The first candlestick is referred to as the "mother bar" or "outside bar," and the second candlestick is the "inside bar."

2. Characteristics:
- The first candlestick is typically smaller and has a narrower range compared to the second candlestick.
- The second candlestick has a larger range and completely engulfs the range of the first candlestick.
- Outside Bars can occur in both uptrends and downtrends.

3. Significance:
- Outside Bar patterns suggest a decisive shift in market sentiment, where the momentum of the second candlestick overwhelms that of the first candlestick.
- They indicate a potential reversal of the prevailing trend, with strong buying or selling pressure evident in the engulfing candlestick.
- Outside Bars are considered more significant when they occur at key support or resistance levels or after an extended trend.

4. Trading Strategies:
- **Reversal Trading**: Traders often look for Outside Bar patterns to signal potential reversals in the market. A bullish engulfing pattern (outside bar) after a downtrend or at a key support level could signal a potential reversal to the upside, while a bearish engulfing pattern after an uptrend or at a key resistance level could signal a potential reversal to the downside.
- **Confirmation**: Traders may seek confirmation of Outside Bar patterns through other technical indicators or price action signals, such as volume analysis, trend lines, or support and resistance levels.

5. Risk Management:
- **Stop Loss**: Traders need to place stop-loss orders to manage risk, especially when trading reversal patterns like Outside Bars. This helps limit potential losses if the market moves against the anticipated reversal.

In summary, Outside Bar patterns are valuable tools for identifying potential reversals in the market. While they can provide clear signals of a shift in market sentiment, traders should always consider other factors and use additional confirmation before making trading decisions based solely on Outside Bars.

Chapter 5.4
Harami Candlestick Patterns:

Harami candlestick patterns are significant price action patterns that indicate a potential reversal or consolidation in the market. This pattern consists of two candlesticks, where the second candlestick is completely contained within the range of the first candlestick. Here's a detailed overview:

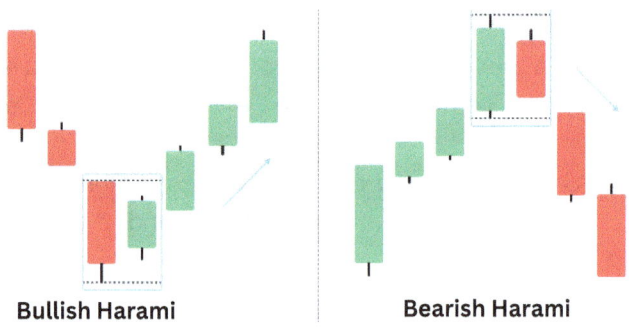

Bullish Harami   Bearish Harami

Harami Candlestick Patterns

1. **Formation**:
- Harami patterns occur when the range (high to low) of the second candlestick is completely contained within the range of the first candlestick. This means that the second candlestick body is smaller than the body of the first candlestick and is completely engulfed by it.
- The first candlestick is typically larger and has a wider range compared to the second candlestick.
- Harami patterns can be bullish or bearish, depending on the direction of the market and the position of the candlesticks.

2. **Characteristics**:
- **Bullish Harami**: The first candlestick is bearish, indicating selling pressure, while the second candlestick is bullish and completely contained within the range of the first candlestick. This suggests a potential reversal from a downtrend to an uptrend.

- **Bearish Harami:** The first candlestick is bullish, indicating buying pressure, while the second candlestick is bearish and completely contained within the range of the first candlestick. This suggests a potential reversal from an uptrend to a downtrend.

3. **Significance**:
- Harami patterns suggest a period of indecision in the market, where the range of the second candlestick is overshadowed by the first candlestick.
- They can signal potential reversals in the market, especially when they occur at key support or resistance levels.
- Harami patterns are more significant when confirmed by other technical indicators or price action signals.

4. **Trading Strategies**:
- **Reversal Trading**: Traders often look for Harami patterns to signal potential reversals in the market. A bullish Harami after a downtrend or at a key support level could signal a potential reversal to the upside, while a bearish Harami after an uptrend or at a key resistance level could signal a potential reversal to the downside.
- **Confirmation**: Traders may seek confirmation of Harami patterns through other technical indicators or price action signals, such as volume analysis, trend lines, or support and resistance levels.

In summary, Harami patterns are valuable tools for identifying potential reversals or consolidations in the market. While they can provide clear signals of indecision or a potential reversal, traders should always consider other factors and use additional confirmation before making trading decisions based solely on Harami patterns.

Chapter 5.5
Kicker Candlestick Pattern:

The Kicker candlestick pattern is a significant reversal pattern in technical analysis, characterized by a sudden and decisive shift in market sentiment. It consists of two candlesticks with opposite colors and significant price gaps between them. Here's a detailed overview:

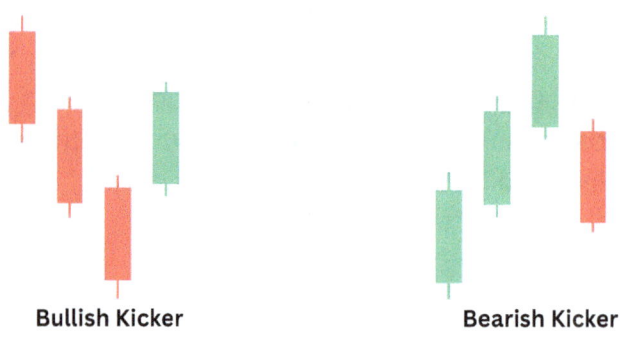

Kicker Candlestick Patterns

1. **Formation**:
- A bullish Kicker pattern occurs after a period of downtrend, while a bearish Kicker pattern occurs after an uptrend.
- The first candlestick in the pattern is in the direction of the prevailing trend and typically has a small body and long shadows (upper and lower wicks).
- The second candlestick is the opposite color of the first candlestick and opens with a significant price gap from the close of the first candlestick. The gap between the two candlesticks is usually large and suggests a sudden change in market sentiment.
- The second candlestick continues in the direction of the reversal, with strong momentum and little to no overlap with the body of the first candlestick.

2. **Characteristics:**
- **Bullish Kicker:** The first candlestick is bearish, and the second candlestick is bullish, opening significantly higher than the close of the first candlestick. This suggests a sudden shift from bearishness to bullishness, with strong buying pressure overpowering previous selling pressure.

- **Bearish Kicker:** The first candlestick is bullish, and the second candlestick is bearish, opening significantly lower than the close of the first candlestick. This suggests a sudden shift from bullishness to bearishness, with strong selling pressure overpowering previous buying pressure.

3. **Significance:**
- Kicker patterns indicate a rapid and decisive change in market sentiment, often accompanied by significant fundamental or news-driven factors.
- They are considered one of the most potent reversal signals in technical analysis due to their clear and decisive nature.
- Kicker patterns are more significant when they occur on higher time frames and are supported by increased trading volume.

4. **Trading Strategies:**
- Reversal Trading: Traders often interpret Kicker patterns as strong signals of trend reversal and may enter positions in the direction of the second candlestick momentum.
- Confirmation: Traders may seek confirmation of Kicker patterns through other technical indicators or price action signals, such as volume analysis, trend lines, or support and resistance levels.

In summary, Kicker patterns are powerful signals of sudden and decisive shifts in market sentiment, often leading to significant price movements. While they can provide clear indications of trend reversals, traders should exercise caution and use additional confirmation before making trading decisions solely based on Kicker patterns.

Chapter 5.6
Abandoned Baby Candlestick Patterns:

The Abandoned Baby candlestick pattern is a significant reversal pattern in technical analysis, indicating a potential reversal in market direction. It consists of three candlesticks and occurs at the end of an uptrend or downtrend. Here's a detailed overview:

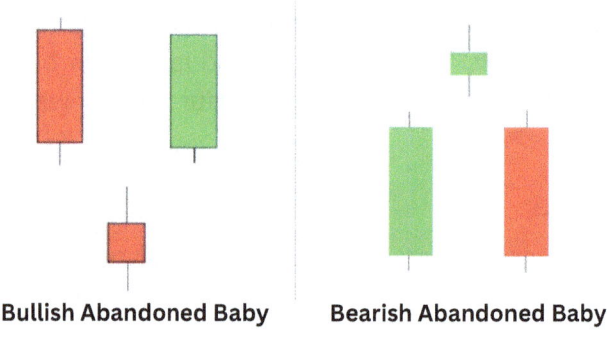

Bullish Abandoned Baby   Bearish Abandoned Baby

Abandoned Baby Candlestick Patterns

1. **Formation**:
- A bullish Abandoned Baby pattern typically occurs at the end of a downtrend, while a bearish Abandoned Baby pattern occurs at the end of an uptrend.
- The pattern begins with a long candlestick in the direction of the prevailing trend.
- The second candlestick is a small-bodied candlestick (either bullish or bearish) that has a price gap away from the previous candlestick, leaving a gap between their bodies.
- The third candlestick is in the opposite direction of the prevailing trend and is typically a long candlestick that closes beyond the opening of the first candlestick, leaving a gap between their bodies.

2. **Characteristics**:
- **Bullish Abandoned Baby**: The first candlestick is bearish, followed by a small-bodied candlestick that gaps lower, leaving a gap between its body and the body of the first candlestick. The third candlestick is bullish, opening higher than the close of the second candlestick and closing beyond the open of the first candlestick.

- **Bearish Abandoned Baby**: The first candlestick is bullish, followed by a small-bodied candlestick that gaps higher, leaving a gap between its body and the body of the first candlestick. The third candlestick is bearish, opening lower than the close of the second candlestick and closing beyond the opening of the first candlestick.

3. **Significance**:
- Abandoned Baby patterns suggest a sudden and significant shift in market sentiment, often caused by fundamental or news-driven factors.
- They are considered strong reversal signals due to their clear indication of a change in market direction.
- Abandoned Baby patterns are more significant when they occur in higher time frames and are supported by increased trading volume.

4. **Trading Strategies**:
- **Reversal Trading**: Traders interpret Abandoned Baby patterns as strong signals of trend reversal and may enter positions in the direction of the third candlestick momentum.
- **Confirmation**: Traders may seek confirmation of Abandoned Baby patterns through other technical indicators or price action signals, such as volume analysis, trend lines, or support and resistance levels.

In summary, Abandoned Baby patterns are potent signals of sudden and decisive shifts in market sentiment, often leading to significant price movements. While they can provide clear indications of trend reversals, traders should exercise caution and use additional confirmation before making trading decisions solely based on Abandoned Baby patterns.

Chapter 6.0 Trading Strategies with Candlestick Patterns
Chapter 6.1
Swing Trading Strategies:

Swing trading, much like a skilled surfer catching waves at just the right moment, involves capturing short- to medium-term price movements within a broader trend. It's akin to riding the waves of market fluctuations, aiming to profit from both upward and downward swings. Let's delve into some effective swing trading strategies.

1. **Identify Trends**: Just as a navigator checks the wind and currents before setting sail, a swing trader must identify prevailing trends. This can be done using technical analysis tools like moving averages, trendlines, or chart patterns. By recognizing the overarching direction of the market, traders can align their positions with the broader trend, increasing the probability of success.

2. **Find Entry and Exit Points**: Successful swing traders, like skilled anglers, patiently wait for the right moment to cast their lines. Entry points are often found near support or resistance levels, where price reversals are likely to occur. Candlestick patterns, such as bullish engulfing or hammer patterns, can also signal opportune entry points. Additionally, employing technical indicators like the Relative Strength Index (RSI) or Stochastic Oscillator can help confirm entry signals. Equally important is defining exit points, whether through profit targets or stop-loss orders, to manage risk and lock in gains.

3. **Risk Management**: Just as a tightrope walker employs safety measures to mitigate risks, swing traders must manage risk effectively. This involves setting stop-loss orders to limit potential losses and adhering to proper position-sizing principles to preserve capital. By maintaining a favorable risk-to-reward ratio, traders can safeguard their portfolios against adverse market movements while maximizing profitability.

4. **Patience and Discipline**: Like a seasoned gardener waiting for seeds to bloom, successful swing traders exercise patience and discipline. Not every trade will result in immediate profits, and it's essential to remain calm and stick to the trading plan even during periods of drawdown. Avoid the temptation to deviate from the strategy based on emotions or short-term fluctuations, as consistency and adherence to the plan are key to long-term success.

5. **Adaptability**: Markets are dynamic and ever-changing, much like the shifting currents of a river. As such, swing traders must remain adaptable and flexible in their approach. This involves continuously monitoring market conditions, adjusting strategies as needed, and being open to new opportunities. Whether it's due to unexpected news events or shifts in market sentiment, the ability to adapt to changing circumstances is critical for sustained success in swing trading.

By combining these strategies with diligent research, ongoing learning, and a commitment to continuous improvement, swing traders can navigate the complexities of the financial markets with confidence and skill. Just as a skilled sailor navigates the open sea, mastering the art of swing trading requires patience, discipline, and a keen understanding of market dynamics.

Chapter 6.2
Day Trading Strategies:

Day trading involves executing trades within the same trading day, aiming to profit from intraday price movements. It requires quick decision-making, discipline, and a solid understanding of market dynamics. Here are some effective day trading strategies.

1. **Scalping**: This strategy involves making numerous small trades throughout the day to capture small price movements. Scalpers aim to capitalize on short-term price fluctuations, often entering and exiting positions within seconds or minutes. By focusing on high-probability setups and tight spreads, scalpers can accumulate profits over multiple trades.

2. **Trend Trading**: Day traders employing trend trading strategies identify prevailing intraday trends and attempt to profit from them. They may use technical indicators such as moving averages, trend lines, or momentum oscillators to confirm trend direction and identify entry and exit points. By aligning trades with the dominant intraday trend, traders increase the likelihood of success.

3. **Breakout Trading**: Breakout traders look for price movements above or below key support or resistance levels. When a stock or market breaks out of a consolidation range or breaches a significant price level, breakout traders enter positions in the direction of the breakout, aiming to capture rapid price movements. Tight stop-loss orders are often used to manage risk in case of false breakouts.

4. **Reversal Trading**: Reversal traders anticipate intraday price reversals and aim to profit from them. This strategy involves identifying overextended moves or exhaustion patterns, such as divergences or candlestick reversal patterns, and entering trades in the opposite direction of the prevailing trend. Reversal traders must exercise caution and wait for confirmation signals to avoid entering prematurely.

5. **Range Trading**: Range traders capitalize on sideways or range-bound markets by buying near support levels and selling near resistance levels. They aim to profit from the price oscillations within a defined trading range. Range trading requires patience and discipline, as traders must wait for clear signals of support or resistance before entering positions.

6. **News-Based Trading**: Day traders may also capitalize on significant news events or earnings releases that cause volatile price movements. By staying informed and reacting quickly to news catalysts, traders can exploit short-term price fluctuations driven by market sentiment. However, news-based trading carries increased risk due to heightened volatility and unpredictable market reactions.

Regardless of the chosen strategy, successful day trading requires strict risk management, discipline, and continuous learning. Traders should develop a comprehensive trading plan, adhere to predefined entry and exit criteria, and constantly evaluate their performance to identify areas for improvement. Additionally, staying informed about market developments, maintaining emotional control, and practicing proper position sizing are essential for long-term success in day trading.

Chapter 6.3
Position Trading Strategies:

Position trading is a long-term trading strategy where traders hold positions for weeks, months, or even years, aiming to capture significant trends and maximize profits. Unlike day trading or swing trading, position traders are less concerned with short-term price fluctuations and focus on capturing broader market movements. Here are some effective position trading strategies.

1. **Trend Following**: Position traders often adopt a trend-following approach, aiming to capitalize on established trends in the market. They identify major trends using technical analysis tools such as moving averages, trend lines, or price patterns. Once a trend is identified, position traders enter positions in the direction of the trend and hold them until there are clear signs of trend reversal. Trend following requires patience and discipline, as positions may be held for extended periods to maximize profits.

2. **Fundamental Analysis**: Fundamental analysis plays a crucial role in position trading, especially for longer-term investments. Position traders analyze fundamental factors such as economic indicators, company earnings, industry trends, and geopolitical events to identify undervalued or overvalued assets. By conducting thorough research and assessing the long-term prospects of the underlying assets, position traders aim to make informed investment decisions that align with their outlook for the market.

3. **Diversification**: Position traders often diversify their portfolios to reduce risk and capture opportunities across different asset classes, sectors, or geographic regions. Diversification helps spread risk and minimize the impact of adverse events on the overall portfolio. Position traders may allocate capital to a mix of stocks, bonds, commodities, currencies, and other assets to achieve a balanced and diversified portfolio.

4. **Risk Management**: Effective risk management is critical for position traders to protect capital and preserve wealth over the long term. Position traders use various risk management techniques, such as setting stop-loss orders, limiting position sizes, and maintaining proper asset allocation. By managing risk effectively, position traders can weather market fluctuations and avoid significant losses.

5. **Patience and Discipline**: Position trading requires patience and discipline to withstand short-term market fluctuations and adhere to the long-term investment thesis. Position traders must resist the temptation to react impulsively to short-term market noise and stay focused on their long-term goals. By maintaining a disciplined approach and staying committed to their trading strategy, position traders can capitalize on long-term market trends and achieve their investment objectives.

6. **Continuous Monitoring and Review**: While position trading involves holding positions for extended periods, it's essential for traders to continuously monitor their investments and review their performance regularly. Position traders should stay informed about market developments, reassess their investment thesis periodically, and adjust their portfolio allocations as needed to adapt to changing market conditions.

In summary, position trading is a long-term investment strategy that requires careful analysis, disciplined execution, and a patient approach. By following these strategies and principles, position traders can position themselves to capitalize on long-term market trends and achieve their investment goals.

Chapter 6.4
Combining Candlestick Patterns with Technical Indicators:

Combining candlestick patterns with technical indicators can enhance trading strategies by providing additional confirmation signals and improving the accuracy of trade entries and exits. Here's how you can integrate candlestick patterns with some commonly used technical indicators.

1. **Moving Averages**: Moving averages help smooth out price data and identify the direction of the trend. Combining moving averages with candlestick patterns can provide confirmation of trend direction and potential reversal points. For example, if a bullish candlestick pattern forms near a rising 50-day moving average, it may signal a potential buying opportunity in an uptrend.

2. **Relative Strength Index (RSI)**: The RSI is a momentum oscillator that measures the speed and change of price movements. When combined with candlestick patterns, divergences between the RSI and price action can provide powerful reversal signals. For instance, if a bearish candlestick pattern forms while the RSI is in overbought territory, it may indicate a potential trend reversal to the downside.

3. **MACD (Moving Average Convergence Divergence)**: The MACD is a trend-following momentum indicator that shows the relationship between two moving averages of a security's price. Traders can use MACD crossovers in conjunction with candlestick patterns to confirm trend changes or reversals. For example, a bullish candlestick pattern forming alongside a bullish MACD crossover may signal a strong uptrend continuation.

4. **Bollinger Bands**: Bollinger Bands consist of a middle band (typically a simple moving average) and two outer bands that represent volatility levels. Combining Bollinger Bands with candlestick patterns can help traders identify potential overbought or oversold conditions. For instance, if a bearish candlestick pattern forms near the upper Bollinger Band, it may indicate a potential reversal to the downside.

5. **Volume**: Volume analysis can provide valuable insights into the strength and validity of candlestick patterns. High-volume breakouts or reversals tend to be more reliable than those accompanied by low-volume. Traders can use volume spikes to confirm the significance of candlestick patterns and validate their trading decisions.

6. **Support and Resistance Levels**: Support and resistance levels are key areas on a price chart where buying and selling pressure converge. Combining candlestick patterns with support and resistance levels can help traders identify potential entry and exit points with high probability. For example, a bullish candlestick pattern forming near a significant support level may indicate a favorable buying opportunity.

When combining candlestick patterns with technical indicators, it's essential to consider the overall market context, trend direction, and potential risk factors. Traders should also use proper risk management techniques, such as setting stop-loss orders and position sizing, to mitigate downside risk and protect capital.

Chapter 7.0 Risk Management and Psychological Aspects
Chapter 7.1
Importance of Risk Management in Trading:

Risk management is paramount in trading, serving as the cornerstone of long-term success and capital preservation. Here's why it's crucial.

1. **Preservation of Capital**: Effective risk management techniques safeguard trading capital from substantial losses. By implementing proper risk controls, such as setting stop-loss orders and adhering to position sizing principles, traders limit the amount of capital at risk in each trade. This ensures that a series of losing trades doesn't deplete the trading account, allowing traders to continue participating in the market and capitalize on future opportunities.

2. **Emotional Discipline**: Risk management strategies help traders maintain emotional discipline and prevent impulsive decision-making driven by fear or greed. By defining risk parameters and sticking to predetermined trading rules, traders avoid the detrimental effects of emotional trading, such as revenge trading or overleveraging. This fosters a rational and disciplined approach to trading, leading to more consistent and profitable outcomes over time.

3. **Consistency and Longevity**: Consistent risk management practices are essential for sustaining profitability and longevity in trading. While individual trades may result in profits or losses, it's the overall risk-adjusted return over a series of trades that determines trading success. By managing risk effectively and aiming for positive expectancy, traders can achieve long-term consistency and durability in their trading endeavors.

4. **Adaptability to Market Conditions**: Market conditions are dynamic and ever-changing, requiring traders to adapt their strategies and risk management techniques accordingly. Effective risk management allows traders to adjust position sizes and risk exposure based on prevailing market conditions, such as volatility levels, trend strength, or economic events. This adaptability enables traders to navigate different market environments and capitalize on opportunities while mitigating potential risks.

5. **Protection Against Black Swan Events**: Risk management strategies provide a buffer against unforeseen events or market shocks, commonly referred to as "black swan" events. While these events are rare and unpredictable, they can have a significant impact on financial markets and individual trading positions. By implementing risk controls and diversifying across multiple asset classes, traders can mitigate the impact of black swan events and protect their portfolios from catastrophic losses.

In summary, risk management is integral to trading success, as it helps preserve capital, maintain emotional discipline, achieve consistency, adapt to changing market conditions, and protect against unexpected events. Traders who prioritize risk management as a fundamental aspect of their trading approach are better positioned to navigate the challenges of the financial markets and achieve their long-term goals.

Chapter 7.2
Overcoming Emotional Biases:

Overcoming emotional biases in trading is essential for maintaining discipline, making rational decisions, and achieving long-term success in the markets. Here are some strategies to help mitigate emotional biases.

1. **Awareness and Self-Reflection**: Recognize and acknowledge your emotional biases. Regularly assess your thoughts, feelings, and behaviors while trading. Keep a trading journal to record your trades, emotions, and decision-making process. Reflect on past experiences to identify patterns of emotional bias and areas for improvement.

2. **Develop a Trading Plan**: Create a comprehensive trading plan that outlines your trading strategy, risk management rules, and predefined entry and exit criteria. Having a well-defined plan helps reduce uncertainty and emotional decision-making by providing clear guidelines for trading activities. Stick to your plan and avoid making impulsive decisions based on emotions.

3. **Set Realistic Expectations**: Manage your expectations and accept that losses are an inevitable part of trading. Understand that no trading strategy is perfect, and losses are an inherent risk of participating in the markets. Focus on achieving consistent profitability over the long term rather than chasing unrealistic gains in the short term.

4. **Implement Risk Management**: Implement effective risk management techniques to protect your trading capital and minimize the impact of losses. Set stop-loss orders to limit potential losses on each trade and adhere to proper position sizing principles. By managing risk effectively, you reduce the emotional stress associated with trading and maintain a disciplined approach to risk-taking.

5. **Practice Patience and Discipline**: Cultivate patience and discipline in your trading approach. Avoid the urge to chase after trades or deviate from your trading plan based on impulsive emotions. Stick to your predefined rules and wait for high-probability setups that align with your strategy. Remember that successful trading requires consistency and adherence to a disciplined approach over time.

6. **Use Technology to Automate Decisions**: Utilize technology to automate trading decisions and reduce emotional bias. Implement algorithmic trading systems or trading robots that execute trades based on predefined rules and algorithms. Automated trading removes the emotional component from decision-making, allowing for more objective and systematic trading.

7. **Seek Support and Accountability**: Surround yourself with a supportive trading community or mentorship group. Share your experiences, challenges, and successes with fellow traders who can provide feedback, encouragement, and accountability. Having a support network can help you stay motivated, gain valuable insights, and overcome emotional biases in trading.

By implementing these strategies and consistently practicing self-awareness, discipline, and risk management, you can effectively overcome emotional biases in trading and improve your overall performance in the markets. Remember that trading is a journey of continuous learning and self-improvement, and mastering your emotions is a critical step towards achieving long-term success.

Chapter 7.3
Setting Realistic Expectations:

Setting realistic expectations in trading is essential for managing risk, maintaining emotional stability, and achieving long-term success. Here are some key principles to consider when setting expectations.

1. **Understand the Nature of Trading**: Recognize that trading is inherently risky and involves the possibility of both profits and losses. No trading strategy can guarantee success, and losses are a natural part of the process. Set realistic expectations by acknowledging the risks involved and understanding that trading outcomes are probabilistic.

2. **Focus on Consistency Over Time**: Instead of aiming for unrealistic short-term gains, focus on achieving consistent profitability over the long term. Understand that trading success is measured by your ability to generate positive returns over a series of trades, rather than by individual trade outcomes. Set achievable goals that reflect your trading strategy, risk tolerance, and market conditions.

3. **Be Patient and Realistic**: Rome wasn't built in a day, and neither is trading success. Avoid the temptation to chase after quick profits or unrealistic returns. Instead, adopt a patient and realistic approach to trading, understanding that it takes time to develop the skills, experience, and discipline necessary to succeed in the markets. Set incremental goals and milestones to track your progress and celebrate your achievements along the way.

4. **Manage Risk Effectively**: Prioritize risk management and capital preservation in your trading approach. Set clear risk management rules, such as defining your maximum risk per trade or adhering to proper position sizing principles. By managing risk effectively, you protect your trading capital from significant losses and create a solid foundation for long-term growth.

5. **Learn from Experience**: Embrace a growth mindset and view trading as a continuous learning process. Treat losses as valuable learning opportunities and analyze your trades to identify areas for improvement. As you gain experience and refine your trading skills, your expectations may evolve accordingly. Stay open-minded, adaptable, and committed to ongoing self-improvement.

6. **Seek Realistic Returns**: Set realistic expectations for your trading returns based on your risk tolerance, trading style, and market conditions. Avoid overly optimistic or unrealistic return targets that may lead to disappointment or excessive risk-taking. Instead, focus on achieving consistent, sustainable returns that align with your financial goals and objectives.

7. **Stay Disciplined and Resilient**: Discipline and resilience are critical traits for successful traders. Stick to your trading plan, follow your predefined rules, and remain resilient in the face of adversity. Understand that setbacks and challenges are inevitable in trading, but it's how you respond to them that ultimately determines your success. Stay disciplined, stay focused, and stay committed to your long-term goals.

By setting realistic expectations, managing risk effectively, and maintaining discipline and resilience, you can position yourself for long-term success in trading. Remember that trading is a journey, not a destination, and success is measured by your ability to navigate the ups and downs of the markets with patience, perseverance, and determination.

Chapter 8.0
Case Studies:

Certainly! Here are a few real-life examples of successful trades using candlestick patterns.

1. **Bullish Engulfing Pattern**: In a stock exhibiting a downtrend, a bullish engulfing pattern formed at a significant support level. This pattern indicated a potential reversal, with the second candlestick completely engulfing the body of the first candlestick. Traders who recognized this pattern entered long positions, anticipating a reversal. As the price rallied following the bullish engulfing pattern, traders were able to capture profits.

2. **Hammer Pattern**: In a currency pair experiencing a prolonged downtrend, a hammer pattern is formed at a key support level. The long lower shadow of the hammer indicated strong buying pressure and potential exhaustion of the downtrend. Traders who identified this pattern entered long positions, expecting a reversal. As the price reversed and rallied following the hammer pattern, traders profited from the uptrend.

3. **Morning Star Pattern**: In a stock with a sideways trading range, a morning star pattern formed after a period of consolidation. The morning star pattern consisted of three candlesticks: a long bearish candlestick, a small-bodied candlestick, and a long bullish candlestick. Traders who recognized this pattern entered long positions, anticipating a breakout from the trading range. As the price broke out to the upside following the morning star pattern, traders were able to profit from the uptrend.

4. **Bullish Engulfing Pattern on Support**: In a commodity experiencing a pullback within an uptrend, a bullish engulfing pattern formed at a key support level. This pattern indicated a potential continuation of the uptrend, with the second candlestick engulfing the body of the previous bearish candlestick. Traders who identified this pattern entered long positions, expecting the uptrend to resume. As the price rallied following the bullish engulfing pattern, traders captured profits as the uptrend continued.

These are just a few examples of successful trades using candlestick patterns. It's important to note that while candlestick patterns can provide valuable insights into market sentiment and potential price movements, they should be used in conjunction with other technical analysis tools and risk management techniques for optimal trading decisions. Additionally, traders should always conduct thorough analysis and verify patterns with additional confirmation before entering trades based solely on candlestick patterns.

Chapter 9.0
Creating a Trading Plan:

Developing a personalized trading plan incorporating candlestick patterns involves several steps to ensure consistency, discipline, and profitability in your trading approach. Here's a comprehensive guide to help you create your trading plan.

1. **Define Your Trading Goals and Objectives**:
- Determine your financial goals, risk tolerance, and time horizon for trading.
- Set specific, measurable, achievable, relevant, and time-bound (SMART) trading goals that align with your objectives.

2. **Choose Your Trading Style**:
- Identify your preferred trading style based on your personality, lifestyle, and available time for trading.
- Common trading styles include day trading, swing trading, and position trading.

3. **Select Tradable Assets and Markets**:
- Decide which financial instruments and markets you want to trade, such as stocks, forex, commodities, or cryptocurrencies.
- Consider factors like liquidity, volatility, and trading hours when selecting assets.

4. **Learn Candlestick Patterns**:
- Familiarize yourself with different candlestick patterns and their interpretations.
- Study the characteristics, formations, and significance of popular candlestick patterns, such as doji, engulfing, hammer, and morning star patterns.

5. **Identify Key Technical Indicators**:
- Determine which technical indicators complement your trading strategy and align with candlestick patterns.
- Common indicators include moving averages, RSI, MACD, Bollinger Bands, and volume.

6. **Develop Entry and Exit Criteria**:
- Define clear entry signals based on candlestick patterns, technical indicators, and other factors.
- Establish criteria for setting stop-loss orders, take-profit targets, and trailing stops to manage risk and optimize reward-to-risk ratios.

7. **Create Risk Management Rules**:
- Set rules for position sizing, risk per trade, and maximum drawdown to protect your trading capital.
- Determine the percentage of your capital you are willing to risk on each trade and adjust position sizes accordingly.

8. **Backtest Your Strategy**:
- Backtest your trading strategy using historical data to evaluate its performance and profitability.
- Analyze the results to identify strengths, weaknesses, and areas for improvement.

9. **Demo Trade and Refine Your Plan**:
- Practice trading your strategy in a demo account to gain experience and confidence.
- Make adjustments to your plan based on your demo trading results and real-time market observations.

10. **Monitor Your Progress and Review Your Plan Regularly**:
- Keep track of your trading performance, including win rate, average gain, average loss, and overall profitability.
- Review your trading plan periodically to ensure it remains relevant and effective in different market conditions.

By following these steps and developing a personalized trading plan incorporating a candlestick pattern, you can increase your chances of success in the financial markets while minimizing risks and maximizing profits. Remember that consistency, discipline, and continuous learning are essential for long-term trading success.

Chapter 10.0 Conclusions
Chapter 10.1
Summary of Key Points:

In summary, here are the key points to consider when trading candlestick patterns.

1. **Understanding Candlestick Patterns**: Candlestick patterns are graphical representations of price movements that can help traders identify potential reversals, continuations, or indecision in the market.

2. **Types of Candlestick Patterns**: There are numerous candlestick patterns, including reversal patterns like engulfing patterns, hammer patterns, and morning/evening star patterns, as well as continuation patterns like flags, pennants, and triangles.

3. **Significance of Candlestick Patterns**: Candlestick patterns provide valuable insights into market sentiment and potential price movements. However, they should be used in conjunction with other technical analysis tools and confirmation signals for optimal trading decisions.

4. **Confirmation and Validation**: It's essential to validate candlestick patterns with other technical indicators, trend analysis, volume analysis, and support/resistance levels before entering trades based solely on candlestick patterns.

5. **Risk Management**: Effective risk management is crucial when trading candlestick patterns to protect capital and minimize losses. Implement proper position sizing, set stop-loss orders, and adhere to risk management rules to manage risk effectively.

6. **Backtesting and Practice**: Before trading with real money, backtest your trading strategy incorporating candlestick patterns using historical data to evaluate its performance. Practice trading in a demo account to gain experience and confidence before transitioning to live trading.

7. **Continuous Learning and Adaptation**: Markets are dynamic, and candlestick patterns may behave differently in various market conditions. Continuously educate yourself, stay updated with market developments, and be willing to adapt your trading strategy as needed.

8. **Patience and Discipline**: Patience and discipline are essential virtues for successful trading. Stick to your trading plan, avoid emotional decision-making, and maintain consistency in your approach to trading candlestick patterns.

By keeping these key points in mind and incorporating them into your trading strategy, you can effectively utilize candlestick patterns to make informed trading decisions and improve your overall performance in the financial markets.

Chapter 10.2
Encouragement to Continue Learning and Practicing:

Absolutely! Here's some encouragement to keep learning and practicing candlestick patterns.

1. **Knowledge is Power**: The more you know about candlestick patterns, the better equipped you are to navigate the complexities of the financial markets. Each pattern tells a story about market sentiment and potential price movements, empowering you to make informed trading decisions.

2. **Continuous Improvement**: Trading is a journey of continuous learning and self-improvement. By dedicating yourself to learning and practicing candlestick patterns, you're investing in your skills and abilities as a trader. Every bit of knowledge gained and every trade executed brings you one step closer to achieving your trading goals.

3. **Unlocking Opportunities**: Candlestick patterns provide valuable insights into market dynamics and potential trading opportunities. By mastering these patterns, you can identify high-probability setups, anticipate market reversals, and capitalize on trends, giving you a competitive edge in the markets.

4. **Building Confidence**: Knowledge breeds confidence. As you become more proficient in identifying and interpreting candlestick patterns, you'll gain confidence in your trading decisions and ability to navigate the markets effectively. Confidence is a key ingredient for success in trading, helping you stay focused and disciplined even in challenging market conditions.

5. **Adaptability to Market Changes**: Markets are constantly evolving, and what works today may not work tomorrow. By staying updated with new candlestick patterns, variations, and market developments, you enhance your adaptability and ability to thrive in changing market environments.

6. **Joining a Community of Traders**: Learning candlestick patterns opens the door to a vibrant community of traders who share knowledge, insights, and experiences. By connecting with fellow traders, you can exchange ideas, learn from each other's successes and mistakes, and grow together as traders.

7. **The Thrill of Mastery**: There's a sense of satisfaction and fulfillment that comes from mastering a skill. As you become proficient in identifying and trading candlestick patterns, you'll experience the thrill of watching your trading performance improve and your account grow. Embrace the journey and celebrate every milestone along the way.

Remember, learning and practicing candlestick patterns is not just about making profits; it's about honing your craft, expanding your horizons, and fulfilling your potential as a trader. So, keep studying, keep practicing, and keep striving for excellence. The journey may have its challenges, but the rewards are well worth it. Happy trading!

Appendix I
Glossary of Terms:

Certainly! Here's a glossary of terms commonly used in candlestick patterns trading.

1. **Candlestick**: A graphical representation of price movements within a specific period, typically displaying open, high, low, and closed prices.

2. **Bullish**: A term used to describe price movements indicating upward momentum or optimism in the market.

3. **Bearish**: A term used to describe price movements indicating downward momentum or pessimism in the market.

4. **Reversal Pattern**: A candlestick pattern that suggests a potential reversal in the prevailing trend, signaling a shift in market sentiment.

5. **Continuation Pattern**: A candlestick pattern that suggests a continuation of the prevailing trend, indicating a temporary pause before the trend resumes.

6. **Doji**: A candlestick pattern with a small real body, indicating indecision or a standoff between buyers and sellers.

7. **Engulfing Pattern**: A candlestick pattern where the body of one candle completely engulfs the body of the previous candle, signaling a potential reversal in the trend.

8. **Hammer**: A bullish candlestick pattern characterized by a small body and a long lower shadow, indicating strong buying pressure after a decline.

9. **Shooting Star**: A bearish candlestick pattern characterized by a small body and a long upper shadow, indicating strong selling pressure after an uptrend.

10. **Morning Star**: A bullish candlestick pattern consisting of three candles: a long bearish candle, a small-bodied candle, and a long bullish candle, signaling a potential reversal from a downtrend to an uptrend.

11. **Evening Star**: A bearish candlestick pattern similar to the morning star, but occurring at the end of an uptrend, signaling a potential reversal from an uptrend to a downtrend.

12. **Marubozu**: A candlestick pattern with a long body and little to no shadows, indicating strong buying or selling pressure depending on whether it's bullish or bearish.

13. **Piercing Pattern**: A bullish candlestick pattern formed by two candles, with the second candle opening below the low of the first candle and closing above the midpoint of the first candle's body.

14. **Dark Cloud Cover**: A bearish candlestick pattern formed by two candles, with the second candle opening above the high of the first candle and closing below the midpoint of the first candle's body.

15. **Harami**: A candlestick pattern consisting of two candles, with the second candle fully contained within the range of the first candle, indicating a potential reversal.

16. **Bullish/Bearish Engulfing**: A bullish engulfing pattern occurs when a small bearish candlestick is followed by a larger bullish candlestick that completely engulfs the body of the previous candlestick. A bearish engulfing pattern is the opposite, where a small bullish candlestick is followed by a larger bearish candlestick that completely engulfs the body of the previous candlestick.

17. **Tweezer Tops/Bottoms**: A candlestick pattern formed by two candles with equal or near-equal highs (tweezer tops) or lows (tweezer bottoms), indicating potential reversal points.

18. **Inside Bar**: A candlestick pattern where the range of the current candle is completely within the range of the previous candle, suggesting consolidation or indecision in the market.

19. **Outside Bar**: A candlestick pattern where the range of the current candle exceeds the range of the previous candle, often signaling a potential reversal or continuation of the trend.

20. **Gap**: A price gap occurs when there is a significant difference between the closing price of one candlestick and the opening price of the next candlestick, indicating a sudden shift in market sentiment.

These are just a few of the key terms used in candlestick patterns trading. Familiarizing yourself with these terms will help you better understand and interpret candlestick patterns, enabling you to make more informed trading decisions.

Appendix II
Legal Disclaimer:

The information provided in this book is for general informational and educational purposes only and is not a substitute for professional advice. The author and publisher have made every effort to ensure the accuracy of the information within this book, but they make no representations or warranties regarding the completeness, accuracy, reliability, suitability, or availability of the content. Any reliance you place on such information is therefore strictly at your own risk.

Professional Advice Disclaimer:
This book does not contain or constitute, and should not be interpreted as, financial, investment, legal, or other professional advice. The content is intended to be used for informational purposes only. You should consult with a professional to determine what may be best for your individual needs.

No Guarantees:
The author and publisher disclaim any responsibility for any liability, loss, or risk incurred as a consequence, directly or indirectly, from the use and application of any of the contents of this book. There are no guarantees of any results or outcomes based on the information provided.

Personal Responsibility:
You acknowledge that you are voluntarily participating in the use of this book and that you are solely and personally responsible for your choices, actions, and results, now and in the future. You accept full responsibility for the consequences of your use or non-use of any information provided in this book, and you agree to use your own judgment and due diligence before implementing any idea, suggestion, or recommendation from this book.

Limitation of Liability:
In no event will the author, publisher, or any of their affiliates, be liable for any loss or damage including without limitation, indirect or consequential loss or damage, or any loss or damage whatsoever arising from reliance on the information provided in this book.

External Links:
This book may contain links to external websites that are not provided or maintained by or in any way affiliated with the author. Please note that the author does not guarantee the accuracy, relevance, timeliness, or completeness of any information on these external websites.

Copyright Notice:
All rights reserved. No part of this book may be reproduced, distributed, or transmitted in any form or by any means, including photocopying, recording, or other electronic or mechanical methods, without the prior written permission of the author, except in the case of brief quotations embodied in critical reviews and certain other noncommercial uses permitted by copyright law.

For permission requests, please contact the author at the following address:
Elio Vazquez
7990 SW 117th Ave, Suite 133
Miami, FL 33183-3845
support@eliovazquez.com
www.eliovazquez.com

Contact Information:
If you have any questions about this book, please contact the author at support@eliovazquez.com

www.ingramcontent.com/pod-product-compliance
Lightning Source LLC
Chambersburg PA
CBHW070301230526
45470CB00002B/670